Test Your Higher Chemistry Calculations

by

David Calder

Cover graphic by Sharon Colman

ISBN 0 7169 3211 3

ROBERT GIBSON · Publisher
17 Fitzroy Place, Glasgow, G3 7SF, Scotland, U.K.

INTRODUCTION

Calculations take up a significant part of the Higher Chemistry syllabus and contribute approximately 20% of the total marks in the examination.

However, calculations appear in many different sections of the work and within any section there can be a large range of type of question and level of difficulty of problem. As a result and in the short teaching time available it can often be very difficult for students to get adequate practice in all the possible types of calculation question which might appear in the examination. Perhaps not surprisingly, a recent examination report stated that "often there was little or no attempt at calculations" and this could result in many candidates not fulfilling their expectations of a pass or a high award.

This book is intended to address the difficulties which students have with this important area of Chemistry. It contains 18 chapters covering all the types of calculation likely to be met in Higher Chemistry. Each chapter contains a brief outline of necessary theory, followed by worked examples showing how to tackle the different types of calculation and enough problems to give students plenty of practice at applying the knowledge and methods involved. Answers are provided to allow students to check their own work. This will enable students to work at their own rates, building up confidence as they progress through each topic.

All the material contained in this book has been successfully used with my own Higher students over several years. I hope that you will also find it useful and discover that this aspect of Chemistry is not as difficult or intimidating as you thought.

All the best with your studies!

David Calder, December 1996

CONTENTS

1. RELATIVE ATOMIC MASS

The relative atomic mass (also known as the atomic weight) of an element is the **average mass** of an atom in a sample of the pure element. This average takes account of the masses of the different isotopes present and their relative abundances (amounts).

An example of what this means can be seen in the very simplified picture below which represents a sample of copper containing 10 atoms. Copper has two isotopes, of masses 63 and 65, and they are present in the approximate proportions shown.

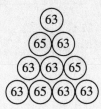

The average mass of an atom is calculated by obtaining the total mass of the sample and dividing it by the number of atoms in the sample as below.

7 atoms each have a mass of 63. Total: $7 \times 63 = $ **441**

3 atoms each have a mass of 65. Total: $3 \times 65 = $ **195**

10 atoms have a total mass of: **636**

Average mass of 1 atom $= \dfrac{636}{10} = $ **63.6**

So the relative atomic mass of copper, calculated from the above simplified data, is 63.6.

The above calculation, involving a sample of 10 atoms, is a very simple illustration of what is meant by relative atomic mass. More usually, however, the amounts of the isotopes present are given as **percentage abundances**. In such cases, it is convenient to imagine a sample of 100 atoms, as in the following Worked Examples.

WORKED EXAMPLE 1.1

Calculate the relative atomic mass of copper from the data given below.

Mass of isotope	Relative abundance
63	69%
65	31%

If we consider an imaginary "sample" of 100 atoms, then:

69 atoms each weigh 63. Total: $69 \times 63 = 4347$

31 atoms each weigh 65. Total: $31 \times 65 = 2015$

100 atoms have a total mass of: **6362**

Average mass of 1 atom $= \dfrac{6362}{100} = $ **63.62**

So the relative atomic mass of copper is 63·6 rounded to 3 significant figures.

WORKED EXAMPLE 1.2

Neon has three isotopes with relative abundances as shown below.

Mass of isotope	Relative abundance
20	90·9%
21	0·3%
22	8·8%

Calculate the relative atomic mass of neon from the data given.

A difference between this and the previous example is that the percentage abundances are not whole numbers. However, we proceed as before, imagining a sample of 100 atoms, and ignoring the fact that you can't actually get fractions of atoms, as in 90·9, 0·3 etc!

$$90 \cdot 9 \text{ atoms each weigh 20. Total: } 90 \cdot 9 \times 20 = 1818$$
$$0 \cdot 3 \text{ atoms each weigh 21. Total: } 0 \cdot 3 \times 21 = 6 \cdot 3$$
$$8 \cdot 8 \text{ atoms each weigh 22. Total: } 8 \cdot 8 \times 22 = 193 \cdot 6$$

100 atoms have a total mass of: **2017·9**

So the average mass of 1 atom is $\dfrac{2017 \cdot 9}{100}$ = **20·179**

So, the relative atomic mass of neon is 20·2, rounded to 3 significant figures.

WORKED EXAMPLE 1.3

A pure sample of an element was analysed by mass spectrometer and the following chart was obtained. The chart is *not* drawn to scale.

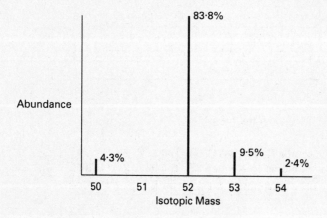

Calculate the relative atomic mass of the element from the above data.

There is no difference between this and earlier Worked Examples except that the data appears in the form of a chart. We proceed as before, assuming that we have a sample of 100 atoms of the element.

$$
\begin{array}{llll}
\text{4·3 atoms each weigh 50. Total:} & 4·3 \times 50 & = & 215 \\
\text{83·8 atoms each weigh 52. Total:} & 83·8 \times 52 & = & 4357·6 \\
\text{9·5 atoms each weigh 53. Total:} & 9·5 \times 53 & = & 503·5 \\
\text{2·4 atoms each weigh 54. Total:} & 2·4 \times 54 & = & 129·6 \\
\end{array}
$$

100 atoms have a total mass of: **5205·7**

So the average mass of 1 atom is $\dfrac{5205·7}{100}$ = **52·057**

So the relative atomic mass of the element is 52·1, rounded to 3 significant figures.

PROBLEMS 1.1 TO 1.15

These problems are of the type shown in Worked Examples 1.1 to 1.3.

1.1 Lithium has two isotopes with masses and relative abundances as shown in the table below.

Mass	Abundance
6	7·4
7	92·6

Calculate the relative atomic mass of lithium from the data given.

1.2 Boron has two isotopes, with relative abundances given in brackets; ^{10}B (18·7%) and ^{11}B (81·3%). Calculate the relative atomic mass of boron from the data given.

1.3 Potassium has two main isotopes with the following mass numbers and abundances. (A third, radioactive, isotope exists, but in such small amounts that it can be ignored for the purposes of this problem.)

Mass	Abundance
39	93·1
41	6·9

Calculate the relative atomic mass of potassium from the above data.

1.4 Vanadium has the following two isotopes, with abundances given in brackets; ^{50}V (0·25%) and ^{51}V (99·75%). Calculate the relative atomic mass of vanadium from the data given.

1.5 50·5% of a pure sample of bromine consists of the isotope ^{79}Br; the other 49·5% consists of ^{81}Br. Calculate the relative atomic mass of bromine using the data given.

1.6 Consider the mass spectrometer chart below which shows an analysis of a pure sample of nickel. The chart is not shown to scale.

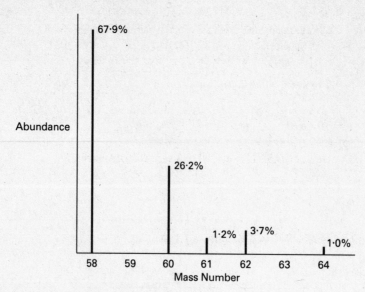

Use the above data to calculate the relative atomic mass of nickel.

1.7 Silicon has three isotopes, with masses and abundances as shown in the table below.

Mass	Abundance
28	92·2%
29	4·7%
30	3·1%

Calculate the relative atomic mass of silicon from the above data.

1.8 Strontium has 4 isotopes, with mass numbers and percentage abundances (given in brackets) as follows: ^{84}Sr (0·5%), ^{86}Sr (9·9%), ^{87}Sr (7·0%) and ^{88}Sr (82·6%). Calculate the relative atomic mass of strontium from this information.

1.9   The mass spectrum of zirconium is shown below.

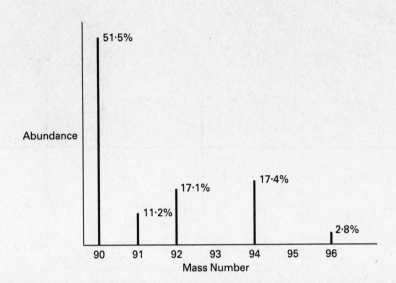

Use the above data to calculate the relative atomic mass of zirconium.

1.10   Argon has 3 isotopes with mass numbers and abundances as given in the table below.

Isotope	Abundance
^{36}Ar	0·34%
^{38}Ar	0·06%
^{40}Ar	99·6%

Calculate the relative atomic mass of argon from the above data.

1.11   The mass spectrometer chart below was obtained from the analysis of a pure sample of tungsten. Use the data given to calculate the relative atomic mass of tungsten. The chart is not to scale.

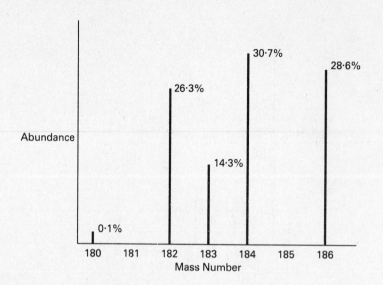

1.12   Cerium has 4 isotopes with masses and percentage abundances as shown in the table below.

Mass	Abundance
136	0·15%
138	0·25%
140	88·5%
142	11·1%

Calculate the relative atomic mass of cerium from the data given.

1.13   Iron has 4 isotopes, with masses and abundances shown in the table below.

Mass	Abundance
54	5·8%
56	91·6%
57	2·2%
58	0·4%

Calculate the relative atomic mass of iron from the data given.

1.14 Lead has 4 isotopes, with masses and abundances shown in the table below.

Isotope	Abundance
^{204}Pb	1·5%
^{206}Pb	23·6%
^{207}Pb	22·6%
^{208}Pb	52·3%

Calculate the relative atomic mass of lead from the data given.

1.15 Palladium has six isotopes with relative abundances as shown in the table below. Use this information to calculate the relative atomic mass of this element.

Isotope	Abundance
^{102}Pd	1 %
^{104}Pd	11 %
^{105}Pd	22·2%
^{106}Pd	27·3%
^{108}Pd	26·7%
^{110}Pd	11·8%

2. THE MOLE: MASSES AND CONCENTRATIONS OF SOLUTIONS

This chapter is in two parts; Part 1 deals with the definition of the mole as a formula mass expressed in grams and Part 2 involves the concentrations of solutions expressed in mol l^{-1} (mol/l). This is a revision of Standard Grade work without any extension to the Higher syllabus.

PART 1: The Mole as a Mass

The definition of a mole as the formula mass of a substance, expressed in grams, should be familiar; this applies, whether the substance is an element or a compound. For example:

$$
\begin{aligned}
1 \text{ mole of Cu} &= 64 \text{ g} \\
1 \text{ mole of } H_2 &= 2 \text{ g} \\
1 \text{ mole of NaCl} &= 58 \cdot 5 \text{ g} \\
1 \text{ mole of } CO_2 &= 44 \text{ g}
\end{aligned}
$$

The worked examples and problems in this chapter should be easy but should not be seen as trivial. They are intended as revision of earlier work and to give practice in setting out arithmetical problems clearly.

WORKED EXAMPLE 2.1

Calculate the mass of 2·5 mol of copper.

The relative atomic mass of Cu = 64.

So 1 mol of Cu $= 64$ g
So 2·5 mol of Cu $= 2 \cdot 5 \times 64$ g
$= \mathbf{160}$ **g**

Note that this initial statement is written this way round, rather than "64 g of Cu = 1 mol" since our answer has to be a number of grams, which we want on the right hand side of the problem.

WORKED EXAMPLE 2.2

How many moles of sodium chloride are present in 11·7 g of the salt?

Formula of sodium chloride is NaCl.
Formula mass of NaCl = 23 + 35·5 = 58·5.
So 1 mole = 58·5 g

Since we want our answer to come out as a number of moles on the right hand side of the problem, we turn the above statement round to give:

58·5 g = 1 mol of NaCl

1 g $= \dfrac{1}{58 \cdot 5}$ mol of NaCl

11·7 g $= \dfrac{11 \cdot 7}{58 \cdot 5}$ mol of NaCl

$= \mathbf{0.2}$ **mol of NaCl**

PROBLEMS 2.1 to 2.20

These problems are of the type shown in Worked Examples 2.1 and 2.2.

2.1   What is the mass of 0.32 mol of calcium nitrate, $Ca(NO_3)_2$?

2.2   How many moles of aluminium carbonate, $Al_2(CO_3)_3$ are present in 4.68 g of the substance?

2.3   How many moles of ammonium carbonate, $(NH_4)_2CO_3$, are present in 115.2 g of the substance?

2.4   What is the mass of 0.025 mol of sucrose, $C_{12}H_{22}O_{11}$?

2.5   Washing soda, sodium carbonate–10–water, has the formula $Na_2CO_3.10H_2O$. How many moles of washing soda are present in 0.715 g of the substance?

2.6   What is the mass of 0.36 mol of ammonium phosphate, $(NH_4)_3PO_4$?

2.7   How many moles of water, H_2O, are present in 5.4 g of the substance?

2.8   What is the mass of 0.08 mol of carbon monoxide, CO?

2.9   How many moles of barium chloride, $BaCl_2$, are present in 3.12 g of the salt?

2.10   What is the mass of 1.2 mol of sodium hydroxide, $NaOH$?

2.11   What is the mass of 0.05 mol of copper(II) chloride, $CuCl_2$?

2.12   How many moles of nitric acid, HNO_3, are present in 94.5 g of the pure substance?

2.13   What is the mass of 0.024 mol of iron(III) oxide, Fe_2O_3?

2.14   How many moles of silver(I) nitrate, $AgNO_3$, are present in 23.8 g of the substance?

2.15   What is the mass of 3.5 mol of propene, C_3H_6?

2.16   How many moles of ammonium sulphate, $(NH_4)_2SO_4$, are present in 105.6 g of the substance?

2.17   What is the mass of 0.6 mol of copper(II) sulphate-5-water, $CuSO_4.5H_2O$?

2.18   How many moles of mercury(II) nitrate, $Hg(NO_3)_2$, are present in 39 g of the substance?

2.19   What is the mass of 0.3 mol of magnesium hydrogencarbonate, $Mg(HCO_3)_2$?

2.20   How many moles of aluminium hydrogensulphite, $Al(HSO_3)_3$, are present in 8.91 g of the substance?

PART 2: The Mole and Concentration

The concentration (or "molarity") of a solution is defined in Chemistry as the number of moles of substance dissolved in every litre of solution; that is, the number of moles per litre. The abbreviation mol l^{-1} is used in this text; the alternative forms of mol/l and M are identical in meaning. For example 0.2 mol l^{-1}, 0.2 mol/l and 0.2 M (0.2 Molar) refer to the same concentration.

In arithmetical terms we describe concentration by the equation:

$$\text{concentration} = \frac{\text{number of moles}}{\text{volume (in litres)}}$$

If we know any two of the above quantities, we can calculate the third. The two other equations derived from the above are:

$$\text{volume (in litres)} = \frac{\text{number of moles}}{\text{concentration}}$$

$$\text{number of moles} = \text{volume (in litres)} \times \text{concentration}$$

WORKED EXAMPLE 2. 3

What is the concentration of a solution containing 2·5 mol of substance dissolved in 5 l of solution?

The appropriate equation is selected and the data put in:

$$\text{concentration} = \frac{\text{number of moles}}{\text{volume (in litres)}}$$

$$= \frac{2 \cdot 5}{5}$$

$$= \textbf{0.5 mol } l^{-1}$$

WORKED EXAMPLE 2.4

How many moles of substance are present in 25 cm^3 of a 0·2 mol l^{-1} solution?

In this problem, the volume of solution has been given in cm^3 and must firstly be converted to litres.

Since 1 l = 1000 cm^3, 25 cm^3 is 25/1000 l = 0·025 l. This value can now be fitted into the appropriate equation:

$$\text{No. of moles} = \text{concentration} \times \text{volume (in litres)}$$
$$= 0 \cdot 2 \times 0 \cdot 025$$
$$= \textbf{0·005 mol}$$

WORKED EXAMPLE 2.5

2 g of sodium hydroxide, NaOH, are dissolved in water to make a 0·4 mol l^{-1} solution. What volume is the solution?

In order to calculate the volume we need to know the concentration and the number of moles, but we are only told the concentration; we must first work out the number of moles of sodium hydroxide from its mass:

Formula of sodium hydroxide: NaOH.
Formula mass: 23 + 16 + 1 = 40.
So 1 mol of NaOH = 40 g.

Reversing this statement, to put "mol of NaOH" on the right hand side, we have:

$$40 \text{ g} = 1 \text{ mol of NaOH}$$

$$1 \text{ g} = \frac{1}{40} \text{ mol of NaOH}$$

$$2 \text{ g} = \frac{2}{40} \text{ mol of NaOH}$$

$$= 0.05 \text{ mol of NaOH}$$

We now fit this value, and that of the concentration, into the appropriate equation:

$$\text{volume (in litres)} = \frac{\text{number of moles}}{\text{concentration}}$$

$$= \frac{0 \cdot 05}{0 \cdot 4}$$

$$= \mathbf{0 \cdot 125 \ } l \ \mathbf{(125 \ cm^3)}$$

WORKED EXAMPLE 2.6

What mass of sodium carbonate, Na_2CO_3, must be dissolved to make 0·25 l of a 0·2 mol l^{-1} solution?

We have the information to calculate the number of moles of sodium carbonate required. This can be fitted into the appropriate equation directly:

No. of moles = concentration × volume (in litres)

= 0·2 × 0·25

= **0·05 mol**

However, the question asks for the **mass** of sodium carbonate which this represents.

Formula of sodium carbonate:	Na_2CO_3,
Formula mass:	2 × 23 + 12 + 3 × 16 = 106
1 mol of sodium carbonate	= 106 g
0·05 mol of sodium carbonate	= 0·05 × 106 g
	= **5·3 g**

PROBLEMS 2.21 to 2.40

■   **Problems 2.21 to 2.25 are of the type shown in Worked Examples 2.3 and 2.4.**
■   **Problems 2.26 to 2.40 are of the type shown in Worked Examples 2.5 and 2.6**

2.21   0·24 mol of salt is dissolved to make 1·2 l of solution. What is the concentration of the solution?

2.22   200 cm^3 of a salt solution has a concentration of 1·5 mol l^{-1}. How many moles of salt are dissolved in it?

2.23   0·005 mol of a substance is dissolved in 25 cm^3 of solution. What is the concentration of the solution?

2.24   What is the volume (in cm^3) of a 1·2 mol l^{-1} solution which contains 0·048 mol of dissolved substance?

2.25   A flask contains 300 cm^3 of a 0·5 mol l^{-1} acid solution. How many moles of pure acid must have been dissolved?

2.26   2·94 g of pure sulphuric acid, H_2SO_4, is dissolved in water to make 150 cm^3 of solution. What is the concentration of the acid solution now?

2.27   A 0·2 mol l^{-1} solution of sodium carbonate, Na_2CO_3, is made by dissolving 5·3 g of the solid in water and making it up to the mark in a standard flask. What volume must the flask be?

2.28   0·8 l of a 0·5 mol l^{-1} solution of ammonium nitrate, NH_4NO_3, has to be made up; what mass of solid ammonium nitrate would be required?

2.29   71 g of sodium sulphate, Na_2SO_4, is dissolved to make a 2 l standard solution. What concentration is the solution?

2.30   25 cm^3 of a 0·4 mol l^{-1} solution of ammonium sulphate, $(NH_4)_2SO_4$, is made up. What mass of solid must have been dissolved?

2.31   A 0·2 mol l^{-1} solution of potassium nitrate, KNO_3, is made by dissolving 30·3 g of the solid in a standard flask. What volume is the standard flask?

2.32   0·4 g of sodium hydroxide, $NaOH$, is dissolved in water to make a 0·25 mol l^{-1} solution. What volume is the solution?

2.33   2·675 g of ammonium chloride, NH_4Cl, is dissolved in water to make a 0·1 mol l^{-1} solution. What volume of solution is made?

2.34   What mass of anhydrous copper(II) sulphate, $CuSO_4$, would be required to make 80 cm^3 of a 0·15 mol l^{-1} solution?

2.35   What would be the concentration of a 300 cm^3 solution of silver(I) nitrate, $AgNO_3$, containing 2·55 g of dissolved solid?

2.36   1·92 g of ammonium carbonate, $(NH_4)_2CO_3$, is dissolved to make 400 cm^3 of solution. What is the concentration of the solution?

2.37   2·76 g of potassium carbonate, K_2CO_3, is dissolved in 200 cm^3 of solution. What is the concentration of the solution?

2.38   What mass of pure ethanoic acid, CH_3COOH, would be required to make 40 cm^3 of a 0·4 mol l^{-1} solution?

2.39   14·3 g of sodium carbonate-10-water, $Na_2CO_3.10H_2O$, is dissolved in water and made up to 250 cm^3 in a standard flask. What is the concentration of the sodium carbonate solution?

2.40   Oxalic acid has the formula $(COOH)_2$. If 0·0225 g of the pure acid was dissolved in water to make a 0·01 mol l^{-1} solution, what would the volume of the solution be?

3. EMPIRICAL FORMULAE

The term **empirical** means "obtained by experiment". Empirical formulae are those calculated from analysing compounds experimentally rather than by referring to electron arrangements.

This chapter is essentially a revision of Standard Grade work, with some extension to more difficult work at the level of Higher Grade. Worked Examples 3.1 to 3.4 are reminders of earlier work; however, Worked Examples 3.5 and 3.6 introduce a new and unfamiliar aspect to the topic.

WORKED EXAMPLE 3.1

A sample of an oxide of copper is found to contain 4 g of copper combined with 0·5 g of oxygen. Calculate its empirical formula.

The first step is to put the information in the form of a table as shown below:

Element:	Cu	O
Actual Mass:	4 g	0·5 g
1 mole:	64 g	16 g

The mass of 1 mole of each element has been entered; note that in the case of oxygen, we are referring to O's (atoms or ions) and not O_2's as if we were referring to oxygen gas. So 1 mole of O weighs 16 g.

We next calculate how many moles of each element we **actually have** in the sample referred to. This is entered in the table as '**Actual Moles**' as shown below.

	Cu	O
Actual Moles:	$\dfrac{4}{64}$	$\dfrac{0·5}{16}$
	= 0.0625	= 0.03125

What we have worked out is the ratio of the number of copper particles to oxygen particles in the compound. The figures look complicated, but if we look carefully, we can see that the 0·0625 figure for Cu is **exactly twice** the 0·03125 figure for O. We can now put this relationship in the table as a "**Whole Number Ratio**".

	Cu	O
Whole no. ratio:	2	1

This means that there are 2 Cu for every 1 O in the copper oxide. So its empirical formula is Cu_2O.

WORKED EXAMPLE 3.2

A sample of chromium oxide is found to contain 68·4% chromium by mass. Calculate the empirical formula of the compound.

In this example, the proportions of the elements present are expressed as percentages. The easiest way to handle this is to imagine that we have 100 g of the chromium oxide. Our "sample" must therefore contain 68·4 g of chromium. Since the only other element present in the compound is oxygen, its mass must be 31.6 g. So we set out the data in a table as before.

Element:	Cr	O
Actual Mass:	68·4 g	31·6 g
1 mole:	52 g	16 g
Actual Moles:	$\dfrac{68\cdot4}{52}$	$\dfrac{31\cdot6}{16}$
	= **1·315***	= **1·975** (* rounded)

This is the ratio of the particles of chromium and oxygen in the compound; the problem here is that there is no immediately obvious whole number ratio. In a situation like this, the most useful approach is to divide both numbers by the smaller.

$$\text{Ratio:} \qquad \frac{1\cdot315}{1\cdot315} \qquad \frac{1\cdot975}{1\cdot315}$$

$$= 1 \qquad\qquad = 1\cdot5$$

The purpose of this was to make the smaller of the numbers in the ratio equal to 1. As long as we multiply or divide both numbers **by the same number**, we will not change the ratio. We still have not got a whole number ratio, but it should be obvious that if we now **multiply both numbers by 2**, we get the whole number ratio as below.

	Cr	O
Whole no. ratio:	2	3

The empirical formula of the compound is therefore Cr_2O_3.

Before leaving this Worked Example, it needs to be noted that when the ratio 1:1·5 was calculated, the second figure did not come out to be 1·5 exactly, but 1·5019. This number was **rounded** to 1·5. Why does it not work out to be **exactly** the kind of simple numbers that we are looking for? The reason is partly that the original figures came from an experiment, and there will always be some error there; also, our original percentage figures may have been rounded. For example, the actual percentage of Cr may have been a figure such as 68·412 % and not the 68·4 % given in the problem. In addition, during the problem, at the "Actual Moles" stage, further rounding took place. As a result, the final ratio may not always work out to contain **exact** whole numbers. Provided that it works out to be very close to a whole number ratio, there is no problem; however, if the ratio is far out from a whole number ratio, look back for a mistake.

WORKED EXAMPLE 3.3

A 0·75 g sample of a hydrocarbon is analysed and found to contain 0·6 g of carbon.

(a) **Calculate its empirical formula.**

(b) **If the molecular mass of the compound is known to be 30, calculate its molecular formula.**

(a) Since we are told that the compound is a hydrocarbon, and therefore only contains the elements carbon and hydrogen, we firstly deduce that the compound contains 0·15 g of hydrogen in addition to the 0·6 g of carbon. We set out the data in a table as before.

Element:	C	H
Actual Mass:	0·6 g	0·15 g
1 Mole:	12 g	1 g
Actual Moles:	$\dfrac{0·6}{12}$	$\dfrac{0·15}{1}$
	= 0·05	= 0·15
Whole no. ratio:	1	3

So the empirical formula is CH_3.

(Note that if the step from Actual Moles to the Whole Number Ratio of 1:3 was not obvious, use the method shown in the previous Worked Example; that is, divide each Actual Moles number by the smaller, in this case 0·05.)

(b) This part of the question states that the molecular mass of the compound is 30 and asks for the *molecular formula*. What we have calculated is the *empirical formula*; this is the simplest whole number ratio of the elements in the compound; it is **not** necessarily the same as the *molecular formula*. **If** there were a compound with the formula CH_3 (which there is not), it would have molecular mass 15. The molecular mass is 30, i.e. twice that figure, so we deduce that **the molecular formula must be C_2H_6.**

WORKED EXAMPLE 3.4

An organic compound is analysed and found to contain, by mass, 38·7% carbon, 9·7% hydrogen and 51·6% oxygen.

(a) **Calculate the empirical formula of the compound.**

(b) **The molecular mass of the compound is 62. Hence, calculate the molecular formula of the compound.**

(a) The only difference between this and previous Worked Examples is that this involves three elements, instead of the two. The method of tackling it is, however, no different from before. The data are set out in a table as below, imagining, as before, that we have a 100 g sample of the compound.

Element:	C	H	O
Actual Mass:	38·7 g	9·7 g	51·6 g
1 Mole:	12 g	1 g	16 g
Actual Moles:	$\dfrac{38·7}{12}$	$\dfrac{9·7}{1}$	$\dfrac{51·6}{16}$
	= 3·225	= 9·7	= 3·225

As before, to obtain (or at least to move towards) a whole number ratio, we divide throughout by the smallest number, in this case 3·225. This gives us the ratio below:

Whole no. ratio: 1   3*   1

(* 3·007...etc. rounded)

Thus the empirical formula of the compound is CH_3O.

(b) **If** the compound had the molecular formula CH_3O, it would have molecular mass 31. Since we are told that the molecular mass is 62, i.e. **twice** that figure, we deduce that the molecular formula must be $C_2H_6O_2$.

Additional Theory

So far, we have not considered how the original information about the masses or percentage masses of elements in compounds is obtained experimentally. We now consider one method which can be used to obtain the masses of the elements present in samples of organic compounds.

The sample of the compound is weighed and then burned in an excess of oxygen. The combustion products (carbon dioxide and water vapour) are drawn, firstly through a container in which the water vapour is condensed, and then through a solution of concentrated alkali which absorbs any carbon dioxide formed. The containers in which the water is condensed and the carbon dioxide is absorbed are weighed before and after the combustion. This gives us the masses of carbon dioxide and water formed. From this information we can calculate the empirical formula of the original compound; this can be seen in the following two Worked Examples. It should be noted, however, that this method of analysis is only of use for compounds which burn completely to form carbon dioxide and water; that is only compounds containing carbon and hydrogen, or carbon, hydrogen and oxygen.

WORKED EXAMPLE 3.5

A sample of a hydrocarbon is burned completely in an excess of oxygen. 7·92 g of carbon dioxide and 4·05 g of water are produced. Calculate:

(a) **the empirical formula of the hydrocarbon**

(b) **the molecular formula of the hydrocarbon given that its molecular mass is 58.**

(a) We know that all the carbon in the carbon dioxide formed has come from the hydrocarbon, so we calculate the mass of carbon as follows:

Fraction of C in $CO_2 = \dfrac{12}{44} = 0·273$ (rounded)

So mass of **C** in 7·92 g of $CO_2 = 0·273 \times 7·92 = \mathbf{2·16\ g}$

The mass of hydrogen in the sample of the hydrocarbon is similarly calculated.

Fraction of H in $H_2O = \dfrac{2}{18} = 0·111$ (rounded)

So mass of **H** in 4·05 g of $H_2O = 0·111 \times 4·05 = \mathbf{0·45\ g}$

We then put the data just calculated into the table below to calculate the empirical formula.

Element:	C	H
Actual Mass:	2·16 g	0·45 g
1 Mole:	12 g	1 g
Actual Moles:	$\dfrac{2·16}{12}$	$\dfrac{0·45}{1}$
	= **0·18**	= **0·45**

Dividing each figure by the smaller, i.e. 0·18, we get:

Ratio: 1 2·5

Multiplying each figure by 2, we have:

Whole No. Ratio: 2 5

Since this is now the simplest whole number ratio of the atoms, the empirical formula of the hydrocarbon is C_2H_5.

(b) If there were a compound with *molecular formula* C_2H_5, it would have a molecular mass of 29. We are told that the hydrocarbon actually has a molecular mass of 58, so we deduce that the molecular formula must be C_4H_{10}.

WORKED EXAMPLE 3.6

0·75 g of a pure organic compound is burned completely in an excess of oxygen to form 1·65 g of carbon dioxide and 0·9 g of water. Calculate the empirical formula of the compound.

We know that all the carbon in the carbon dioxide formed has come from the compound, so we calculate the mass of carbon as follows:

Fraction of C in $CO_2 = \dfrac{12}{44} = 0·273$ (rounded)

So mass of **C** in 1·65 g of $CO_2 = 0·273 \times 1·65 = \mathbf{0·45\ g}$ (rounded)

The mass of hydrogen in the sample of the hydrocarbon is similarly calculated.

Fraction of H in $H_2O = \dfrac{2}{18} = 0·111$ (rounded)

So mass of **H** in 0·9 g of $H_2O = 0·111 \times 0·9 = \mathbf{0·1\ g}$ (rounded)

We have just calculated that the original 0·75 g sample of the organic compound contains 0·45 g of carbon and 0·1 g of hydrogen. This leaves a mass of 0·2 g unaccounted for. This mass can only be oxygen since we are told that the **only** products of the combustion were carbon dioxide and water. (Oxygen is the **only** element which could be present which would not give rise to an additional product. For example, if sulphur were present, sulphur dioxide would be made on combustion.)

So we can set up our empirical formula table as below:

Element:	C	H	O
Actual Mass:	0·45 g	0·1 g	0·2 g
1 Mole:	12 g	1 g	16 g
Actual Moles:	$\dfrac{0·45}{12}$	$\dfrac{0·1}{1}$	$\dfrac{0·2}{16}$
	= **0·0375**	= **0·1**	= **0·0125**

As before, to obtain (or at least to move towards) a whole number ratio, we divide throughout by the smallest number, in this case 0·0125. This gives us the ratio below:

Whole No. Ratio: 3 8 1

Thus the empirical formula of the compound is C_3H_8O.

PROBLEMS 3.1 - 3.30

■   **Problems 3.1 to 3.10 are two-element problems as shown in Worked Examples 3.1, 3.2 and 3.3.**
■   **Problems 3.11 to 3.20 involve three-element compounds as shown in Worked Example 3.4**
■   **Problems 3.21 to 3.30 are of the type shown in Worked Examples 3.5 and 3.6 involving data obtained from combustion experiments.**

3.1   A sample of tin oxide contains 2·38 g of tin combined with 0·64 g of oxygen. Calculate the empirical formula of the compound.

3.2   A hydrocarbon is found to contain 75% carbon by mass. Calculate the empirical formula of the compound.

3.3   Magnesium nitride contains 72% magnesium by mass. Calculate the empirical formula of the compound.

3.4   8·12 g of a hydrocarbon is found to contain 6·72 g of carbon. Calculate

  (a) its empirical formula;
  (b) its molecular formula, given that its molecular mass is 58.

3.5   2·3 g of an oxide of nitrogen is found to contain 0·7 g of nitrogen. Calculate

  (a) the empirical formula of the oxide;
  (b) the molecular formula of the oxide, given that its molecular mass is 92

3.6   An oxide of phosphorus contains approximately 43·7% phosphorus by mass. Calculate the empirical formula of the compound.

3.7   4·88 g of a silane (a compound of silicon and hydrogen) contains 4·48 g of silicon. Calculate

  (a) the empirical formula of the compound;
  (b) the molecular formula of the compound, given that its molecular mass is 122.

3.8   A hydrocarbon contains approximately 85·7% carbon by mass. Calculate

  (a) its empirical formula;
  (b) its molecular formula, given that its molecular mass is 140.

3.9   Aluminium chloride can exist as molecules of molecular mass 267. A 5·34 g sample of the compound is found to contain 1·08 g of aluminium. Calculate

  (a) the empirical formula of the compound
  (b) the molecular formula of the compound.

3.10   A sample of a lead oxide, known as "red lead", is found to contain 12·42 g of lead combined with 1·28 g of oxygen. Calculate the empirical formula of the lead oxide.

3.11   A sample of an organic nitrogen compound is analysed and found to contain 2·1 g of carbon, 2·45 g of nitrogen and 0·7 g of hydrogen. The molecular mass of the compound is known to be 60. Calculate

  (a) the empirical formula of the compound;
  (b) the molecular formula of the compound.

3.12   The composition of a compound, by mass, is Ca (38·7%), P (20%) and O (41·3%). Calculate the empirical formula of the compound.

3.13   A sample of an organic compound is analysed and found to contain 2·25 g of carbon, 3 g of oxygen and 0·375 g of hydrogen. Calculate

  (a) the empirical formula of the compound
  (b)   the molecular formula of the compound, given that its molecular mass is 60.

3.14 A sample of a compound is found to contain 2·875 g of sodium, 4 g of sulphur and 3 g of oxygen. Calculate the empirical formula of the compound.

3.15 A compound of iron is found to have the following composition by mass: Fe (28·6%); C (30·6%); O (40·8%). Calculate its empirical formula.

3.16 A sample of an organic compound is found to contain 0·588 g of carbon, 0·224 g of oxygen and 0·042 g of hydrogen. Calculate the empirical formula of the compound.

3.17 A compound is analysed and found to contain 0·274 g of barium, 0·064 g of sulphur and 0·096 g of oxygen. Calculate the empirical formula of the compound.

3.18 An organic compound of molecular mass 88 is analysed and found to have the following composition by mass: C (54·5%); O (36·4%); H (9·1%). Calculate

    (a) the empirical formula of the compound;
    (b) its molecular formula.

3.19 A sample of an iron compound contains 3·36 g of iron, 2·88 g of oxygen and 0·18 g of hydrogen. Calculate its empirical formula.

3.20 A sample of a compound contains, by mass, 21·8% carbon, 1·2% hydrogen and 77·0% iodine. It has a molecular mass of 330. Calculate

    (a) the empirical formula of the compound;
    (b) the molecular formula of the compound

3.21 A sample of a hydrocarbon is burned completely in excess oxygen to form 9·504 g of carbon dioxide and 2·592 g of water. Calculate the empirical formula of the hydrocarbon.

3.22 0·48 g of an organic compound is burned completely in excess oxygen to form 1·056 g of carbon dioxide and 0·576 g of water. Calculate the empirical formula of the compound.

3.23 1·68 g of a hydrocarbon of molecular mass 84 is burned in an excess of oxygen; 5·28 g of carbon dioxide is produced in the process, in addition to a quantity of water which was not weighed. Calculate

    (a) the empirical formula of the hydrocarbon;
    (b) the molecular formula of the hydrocarbon.

3.24 2·15 g of an organic compound is burned completely in an excess of oxygen to form 5·5 g of carbon dioxide and 2·25 g of water. Calculate the empirical formula of the compound.

3.25 2·8 g of a hydrocarbon of molecular mass 70 is burned completely in excess oxygen, producing 3·6 g of water, in addition to a quantity of carbon dioxide which was not measured. Calculate

    (a) the empirical formula of the compound
    (b) the molecular formula of the compound.

3.26 4·95 g of an organic compound is burned completely in an excess of oxygen to form 9·9 g of carbon dioxide and 4·05 g of water. Calculate the empirical formula of the compound.

3.27 1·224 g of an organic compound is burned completely in an excess of oxygen to form 2·64 g of carbon dioxide and 1·08 g of water. Calculate the empirical formula of the compound.

3.28 0·867 g of an organic compound is burned completely in oxygen to form 1·87 g of carbon dioxide and 0·765 g of water. Calculate the empirical formula of the compound.

3.29 1·755 g of an organic compound is burned completely in oxygen to form 4·158 g of carbon dioxide and 1·701 g of water. Calculate the empirical formula of the compound.

3.30 2·196 g of an organic compound is burned completely in an excess of oxygen, forming 5·544 g of carbon dioxide and 0·972 g of water. Calculate the empirical formula of the compound.

4. GAS DENSITIES AND MOLAR VOLUMES

The density of a substance is the mass of 1 unit of volume of the material. Several different units of density are used, such as g cm^{-3} ("grams per cubic centimetre"), g l^{-1} ("grams per litre"), kg m^{-3} ("kilograms per cubic metre"), etc. In this chapter, only the unit of g l^{-1} will be used.

The equation defining density is:

$$\text{Density} \quad = \quad \frac{\text{Mass of Sample}}{\text{Volume of Sample}}$$

The other two related equations are:

$$\text{Volume of Sample} \quad = \quad \frac{\text{Mass of Sample}}{\text{Density}}$$

$$\text{Mass of Sample} \quad = \quad \text{Volume of Sample} \times \text{Density}$$

Now consider the four gases listed below, with their densities given in units of g l^{-1}. These figures apply at Standard Temperature and Pressure (stp), that is 273K (0 °C) and 1 atmosphere pressure.

Gas	N_2	O_2	CO	He
Density (g l^{-1})	1·25	1·43	1·25	0·179

We can calculate the volume occupied by 1 mole of a gas (the "molar volume") as follows, taking N_2 as an example.

From the density value, we can write:

1·25 g	occupies a volume of	1	l
1 g	occupies a volume of	$\frac{1}{1\cdot25}$	l
28 g (1 mol)	occupies a volume of	$\frac{28}{1\cdot25}$	l

$$= \quad \textbf{22.4 } l$$
(to 3 significant figures)

If the same calculation is carried out for all the gases listed, it is found that they all have approximately the same molar volume, around 22·4 l (at stp). Since the density figures given above only apply at 273K and 1 atmosphere pressure, and since most industrial chemistry involves gases at other temperatures and pressures, the figure of 22·4 l is not a particularly useful one to remember. **What is important, however, is that 1 mole of *any gas* occupies very nearly the same volume when measured under the same conditions of temperature and pressure.**

Calculations involving density figures can be carried out using the "direct variation" method used throughout this book and illustrated in the calculation above. Alternatively, the three quantities used in the example can be linked in the form of the equations below.

$$\text{Molar Volume} \quad \frac{\text{Mass of 1 Mole}}{\text{Density}}$$

$$\text{Mass of 1 Mole} \quad \text{Molar Volume} \times \text{Density}$$

$$\text{Density} \quad \frac{\text{Mass of 1 Mole}}{\text{Molar Volume}}$$

It should be noted that if the density is in units of g l^{-1} (grams per litre) and the mass of 1 mole is expressed in grams, the molar volume must be in units of l (litres).

WORKED EXAMPLE 4.1

Under certain conditions of temperature and pressure, the density of methane, CH_4, is 1·06 g l^{-1}. Calculate the molar volume of the gas under these conditions.

Both methods for tackling this problem will be shown; the first using an equation to connect density, molar volume and the mass of 1 mole, and the second using "direct variation".

Method 1: Using Equations

The appropriate form of the equation is selected and the data inserted.

$$\text{molar volume} = \frac{\text{mass of 1 mole}}{\text{density}}$$

$$= \frac{16}{1·06}$$

$$= \mathbf{15·1}\ l$$
(to 3 significant figures)

Method 2: Using "Direct Variation"

The first step is to turn the density figure into an opening statement with "litres" on the right hand side, since we want our answer to turn out to be a volume.

1·06g	is the mass of	$1\ l$
1g	is the mass of	$\frac{1}{1.06}\ l$
16g (1 mol)	is the mass of	$\frac{16}{1·06}\ l$

$$= \mathbf{15·1}\ l$$
(to 3 significant figures)

WORKED EXAMPLE 4.2

Under certain conditions, sulphur dioxide gas, SO_2, has a molar volume of 26 l. Calculate the density of the gas under these conditions.

Method 1: Using Equations

$$\text{density} = \frac{\text{mass of 1 mole}}{\text{molar volume}}$$

$$= \frac{64}{26}\ g\ l^{-1}$$

$$= \mathbf{2·46}\ g\ l^{-1}$$
(to 3 significant figures)

Method 2: Using "Direct Variation"

26 l	is the volume of	64	g of SO_2 (1 mole)
1 l	is the volume of	$\frac{64}{26}$	g of SO_2

$$= \mathbf{2·46}\ g$$
(to 3 significant figures)

So the density of the gas is 2·46 g l^{-1}

WORKED EXAMPLE 4.3

A gas has a molar volume of 35 l and a density of 0·8 g l^{-1} under certain conditions. Calculate the molecular mass of the gas.

Method 1: Using Equations

$$\text{mass of 1 mole} = \text{density} \times \text{molar volume}$$
$$= 0\text{·}8 \times 35$$
$$= \textbf{28 g}$$

Since the mass of 1 mole of the gas is 28 g, its molecular mass is 28.

Method 2: Using "Direct Variation"

1 l	has a mass of 0·8 g
35 l (1 mole)	has a mass of 35 × 0·8 g
	= 28 g

Since the mass of 1 mole of the gas is 28 g, its molecular mass is 28.

PROBLEMS 4.1 – 4.10

The following problems are of the type illustrated by Worked Examples 4.1, 4.2 and 4.3.

4.1 At 273 K and at atmospheric pressure, chlorine gas, Cl_2, has a density of 3·2 g l^{-1}. Calculate the molar volume of chlorine under these conditions.

4.2 Under certain conditions, oxygen gas, O_2, has a molar volume of 25 l. Calculate the density of the gas under these conditions.

4.3 The industrial production of ammonia by the Haber Process requires nitrogen, N_2, and hydrogen, H_2, at a temperature of 720 K and at 250 atmospheres. Under these conditions, the densities of nitrogen and hydrogen are, respectively, 118 g l^{-1} and 8·53 g l^{-1}. Calculate the molar volume of each gas under these conditions.

4.4 At 273 K and 1 atmosphere, a gas has a molar volume of 22·4 l and a density of 0·71 g l^{-1}. Calculate the molecular mass of the gas.

4.5 Hydrogen sulphide, H_2S, has a molar volume of 65 l under certain conditions. Calculate the density of the gas under these conditions.

4.6 Under certain conditions, neon, Ne, has a density of 0·9 g l^{-1}. Calculate the molar volume of the gas under these conditions.

4.7 A gas has a molar volume of 29·1 l and a density of 2·2 g l^{-1} under certain conditions of temperature and pressure. Calculate the molecular mass of the gas.

4.8 Ethyne, C_2H_2, has a molar volume of 50 l under certain conditions. What will the density of the gas be under these conditions?

4.9 A gaseous hydrocarbon has a molar volume of 17·3 l and a density of 1·735 g l^{-1} at a certain temperature and pressure. Calculate the molecular mass of the gas and hence identify it.

4.10 At 293 K and atmospheric pressure, a diatomic gaseous element has a molar volume of 24·1 l and a density of 1·33 g l^{-1}. Calculate the molecular mass of the gas and hence identify it.

WORKED EXAMPLE 4.4

A 25 cm^3 sample of a gas weighs 0·0221 g. If its molar volume under these conditions is 29·4 l, calculate its molecular mass.

Method 1: Using Equations

The first step is to calculate the density of the gas:

$$\text{density} \quad = \quad \frac{\text{mass}}{\text{volume}}$$

$$= \quad \frac{0·0221}{0·025} \quad \text{(volume changed to } l \text{ from cm}^3)$$

$$= \quad \textbf{0·884 g } l^{-1}$$

We then select the appropriate equation:

mass of 1 mole = molar volume × density

= 29·4 × 0·884

= **26·0 g**
(to 3 significant figures)

So the molecular mass of the gas is 26·0.

Method 2: Using "Direct Variation".

To obtain the mass of 1 mol of the gas, in grams, we need an opening statement with grams on the right hand side.

After converting 25 cm^3 into litres, we have:

0·025 l	is the volume of	0·0221	g of the gas
1 l	is the volume of	$\dfrac{0·0221}{0·025}$	g of the gas
29·4 l (1 mol)	is the volume of	$\dfrac{0·0221 \times 29·4}{0·025}$	g of the gas

$$= \quad \textbf{26·0 g}$$
(to 3 significant figures)

So the molecular mass of the gas is 26·0.

WORKED EXAMPLE 4. 5

The molar volume of carbon dioxide, CO_2, at stp, is 22·4 l. Calculate the mass of a 50 cm^3 sample of the gas under these conditions.

Method 1: Using Equations

$$\text{density} = \frac{\text{mass of 1 mole}}{\text{molar volume}}$$

$$= \frac{44}{22·4} \text{ g } l^{-1}$$

$$= \textbf{1·964 g } l^{-1} \text{ (rounded)}$$

We then put this calculated value for density, and the volume of the sample given, into the equation below.

$$\text{mass} = \text{density} \times \text{volume}$$

$$= 1·964 \times 0·05 \quad \text{(volume changed from cm}^3 \text{ to } l)$$

$$= \textbf{0·0982 g} \text{ (to 3 significant figures)}$$

Method 2: Using "Direct Variation"

22·4 l	is the volume of	44	g of CO_2 (1 mol)
1 l	is the volume of	$\frac{44}{22·4}$	g of CO_2
0·05 l	is the volume of	$\frac{44 \times 0·05}{22·4}$	g of CO_2

$$= \textbf{0·0982 g} \quad \text{(to 3 significant figures)}$$

WORKED EXAMPLE 4.6

The molar volume of nitrogen gas, N_2, is 25 l under certain conditions. What volume would 0·4 g of nitrogen gas occupy under the same conditions?

Method 1: Using Equations

$$\text{density} = \frac{\text{mass of 1 mole}}{\text{molar volume}}$$

$$= \frac{28}{25} \text{ g } l^{-1}$$

$$= \textbf{1·12 g } l^{-1}$$

This calculated value for density, and the mass of the sample given, are put into the equation below.

$$\text{volume} = \frac{\text{mass}}{\text{density}}$$

$$= \frac{0·4}{1·12} \, l$$

$$= \textbf{0·357 } l \quad \text{(to 3 significant figures)}$$

Method 2: Using "Direct Variation"

28 g (1 mol)	is the mass of	25	l of N_2
1 g	is the mass of	$\dfrac{25}{28}$	l of N_2
0.4 g	is the mass of	$\dfrac{25 \times 0.4}{28}$	l of N_2
	=	**0.357**	l (to 3 significant figures)

PROBLEMS 4.11 – 4.20

These problems are of the type illustrated by Worked Examples 4.4, 4.5 and 4.6.

4.11 At 273 K and 1 atmosphere pressure, a 60 cm^3 sample of carbon monoxide, CO, weighs 0.075 g. Calculate its molar volume under these conditions.

4.12 Ethyne, C_2H_2, has a molar volume of 22 l under certain conditions. Calculate the mass of 20 cm^3 of ethyne under these conditions.

4.13 Helium, He, has a molar volume of 54 l under certain conditions. What volume would 0.24 g of helium occupy under the same conditions?

4.14 A 40 cm^3 sample of hydrogen, H_2, weighs 0.0008 g under certain conditions. Calculate the molar volume of hydrogen under these conditions.

4.15 When ammonia, NH_3, is oxidised industrially, as a stage in the production of nitric acid , it is heated to 1200 K at a pressure of 7 atmospheres. Under such conditions, its molar volume is 13.8 l. Calculate the mass of 150 l of the gas at that temperature and pressure .

4.16 Sulphur trioxide, SO_3, has a molar volume of 24 l under certain conditions. Calculate the volume which 0.15 g of the gas would occupy under these conditions.

4.17 A 10 cm^3 sample of xenon, Xe, weighs 0.054 g at room temperature and pressure. Calculate its molar volume under these conditions.

4.18 In the industrial production of sulphur trioxide as a stage in the manufacture of sulphuric acid, sulphur dioxide, SO_2, and oxygen, O_2, are heated to 725 K at atmospheric pressure. Under these conditions, the sulphur dioxide and oxygen have molar volumes of 58.2 l and 59.5 l respectively. Calculate the mass of 1000 l of each gas under these conditions.

4.19 Butane, C_4H_{10}, has a molar volume of 32 l under certain conditions of temperature and pressure. Calculate the volume which 0.045 g of the gas would occupy under the same conditions.

4.20 A 100 cm^3 flask is filled with carbon dioxide, CO_2, at room temperature and pressure. The mass of the gas in the flask is found to be 0.181 g. Calculate the molar volume of the gas under these conditions.

WORKED EXAMPLE 4.7

Carbon dioxide has a molar volume of 32 l under certain conditions of temperature and pressure. 50 cm³ of a sample of an unknown monatomic gas under the same conditions weighed 0·0625 g. Calculate the atomic mass of the gas and, hence, identify it.

We are told the molar volume of carbon dioxide and asked about another gas under the same conditions. The assumption that we need to make is that **both gases have the same molar volume under the same conditions.** So we can say that the molar volume of the unknown gas is also 32 l.

We proceed as below.

Method 1: Using Equations

We have the information to calculate the density of the gas.

$$\text{density} = \frac{\text{mass}}{\text{volume}}$$

$$= \frac{0 \cdot 0625}{0 \cdot 05} \quad \text{(volume changed to } l \text{ from cm}^3)$$

$$= \mathbf{1 \cdot 25 \text{ g } } l^{-1}$$

We then use this, and the molar volume in the appropriate equation:

$$\text{mass of 1 mole} = \text{molar volume} \times \text{density}$$

$$= 32 \times 1 \cdot 25$$

$$= \mathbf{40 \text{ g}}$$

The only monatomic gases are the Noble Gases; **Argon**, with a relative atomic mass of 40, is the only one which fits the data.

Method 2: Using "Direct Variation"

We start with the same assumption used in the first method, namely that the molar volume of our unknown gas is the same as that of carbon dioxide under the same conditions, that is, 32 l.

We want to obtain the atomic mass of the gas; another way of saying this is that we want to know the mass of 1 mol of the gas (e.g. if the atomic mass is 15, then the mass of 1 mol will be 15 g). So we start with a statement which will make our answer come out as a mass on the right hand side of the problem.

After firstly converting our 50 cm³ into litres, we have:

0·05 l	has a mass of	0·0625	g
1 l	has a mass of	$\dfrac{0 \cdot 0625}{0 \cdot 05}$	g
32 l (1 mol)	has a mass of	$\dfrac{32 \times 0 \cdot 0625}{0 \cdot 05}$	g

$$= \mathbf{40 \text{ g}}$$

Our conclusion is the same as for Method 1. The only monatomic gas (Noble Gas) with a relative atomic mass of 40 is **argon**.

PROBLEMS 4.21 – 4.25

The following problems are of the type illustrated by Worked Example 4.7.

4.21 At 1000 K and under a pressure of 2 atmospheres, nitrogen, N_2, has a density of $0 \cdot 68$ g l^{-1}.

  (a)   Calculate the molar volume of nitrogen under these conditions.
  (b)   Calculate the densities of oxygen and carbon dioxide under the same conditions.

4.22 50 cm^3 of ethane, C_2H_6, weighs $0 \cdot 0625$ g; calculate the molar volume of the gas under these conditions. Under the same conditions 50 cm^3 of an unknown gas is found to weigh $0 \cdot 0792$ g. Calculate the molecular mass of the unknown gas.

4.23 Under certain conditions, a 200 cm^3 sample of oxygen, O_2, weighs $0 \cdot 358$ g. A 400 cm^3 sample of a gas, X, weighs $0 \cdot 354$ g under the same conditions. Calculate the molecular mass of X.

4.24 A 200 cm^3 sample of hydrogen sulphide, H_2S, weighs $0 \cdot 268$ g. Under the same conditions of temperature and pressure, 40 cm^3 of an unknown gas weighed $0 \cdot 05$ g. Calculate the molecular mass of the unknown gas.

4.25 A 20 cm^3 sample of krypton, Kr, weighs $0 \cdot 0672$ g. What mass would a 50 cm^3 sample of argon, Ar, have under identical conditions of temperature and pressure?

5. THE AVOGADRO CONSTANT AND THE MOLE

The term "mole" meaning the "formula mass" of a substance, expressed in grams should already be familiar. In this section, we consider the mole as an actual **number** of particles — called the Avogadro Constant.

Consider 1 mole of each of the following elements:

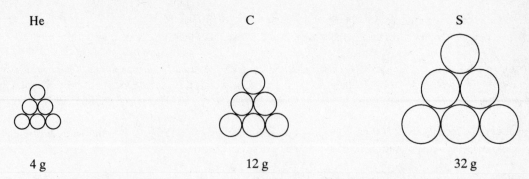

He	C	S
4 g	12 g	32 g

It is convenient for the purpose of this discussion to picture each of the above quantities as a pile of atoms, ignoring the normal structure of the elements.

Now consider **1 atom** of each of these elements, writing their masses in "atomic mass units" (amu). (Note that, strictly speaking, atomic masses are **relative** atomic masses with no unit. However, the use of "amu" may help the understanding of the point being made here.)

He	C	S
4 amu	12 amu	32 amu

Look at the pile of atoms representing 1 mole of He, and weighing 4 g. If 1 atom of He weighs 4 amu, a moment's thought tells us that the number of atoms in the pile is equal to the number of times that 4 amu goes into 4 g. That is:

$$\text{Number of atoms of He in 1 mole} \quad = \quad \frac{4 \text{ g}}{4 \text{ amu}} \quad = \quad \frac{1 \text{ g}}{1 \text{ amu}}$$

Applying the same thinking to the piles of carbon and sulphur atoms, each pile representing 1 mole of the element, we can say that:

$$\text{Number of atoms of C in 1 mole} \quad = \quad \frac{12 \text{ g}}{12 \text{ amu}} \quad = \quad \frac{1 \text{ g}}{1 \text{ amu}}$$

$$\text{Number of atoms of S in 1 mole} \quad = \quad \frac{32 \text{ g}}{32 \text{ amu}} \quad = \quad \frac{1 \text{ g}}{1 \text{ amu}}$$

In each of the above cases, **the number of atoms in a mole of the element is the same**. Its actual value has been calculated to be $6 \cdot 02 \times 10^{23}$ (to 3 significant figures) and is known as the Avogadro Constant, symbol L. Its formal unit is mol^{-1} which should be interpreted as "(particles) per mol".

As stated above, we can now use the term "mole" to mean an actual number of particles, with a numerical value of $6 \cdot 02 \times 10^{23}$. However, as will be seen, great care must be taken to specify the particular type of particle that we are referring to. For example, the word "dozen" refers to an actual number, but it is clear that "a dozen hydrogen atoms" is different from "a dozen hydrogen molecules". (The former has an atomic mass of 12 and contains 12 H atoms; the latter has a molecular mass of 24 and contains 12 H_2 molecules, equal to a total of 24 H atoms.) Similarly, if we refer to a "mole of hydrogen" we must be very careful to say whether we mean hydrogen atoms or molecules.

Consider the following examples carefully to ensure that this point is clear.

1 mol of C	contains	$6 \cdot 02 \times 10^{23}$ **atoms** of C
1 mol of H_2	contains	$6 \cdot 02 \times 10^{23}$ **molecules** of H_2
	contains	$12 \cdot 04 \times 10^{23}$ **atoms** of H
1 mol of CO_2	contains	$6 \cdot 02 \times 10^{23}$ **molecules** of CO_2
	contains	$6 \cdot 02 \times 10^{23}$ **atoms** of C
	contains	$12 \cdot 04 \times 10^{23}$ **atoms** of O
1 mol of $CaCl_2$	contains	$6 \cdot 02 \times 10^{23}$ Ca^{2+} **ions**
	contains	$12 \cdot 04 \times 10^{23}$ Cl^- **ions**
	contains	$18 \cdot 06 \times 10^{23}$ **ions** in total
1 mol of Ne	contains	$6 \cdot 02 \times 10^{23}$ Ne **atoms**
	contains	$60 \cdot 2 \times 10^{23}$ **protons**

(since each Ne atom contains 10 protons)

Note: In the above examples, the usual convention about writing numbers in Standard Form with a number between 1 and 10 multiplied by 10 to some power has been ignored to make comparison between the numbers easier. For example, $12 \cdot 04 \times 10^{23}$ is written rather than $1 \cdot 204 \times 10^{24}$. In all future examples, however, the usual convention will be observed.

WORKED EXAMPLE 5.1

How many atoms are present in $0 \cdot 3$ mol of ammonia, NH_3?

We start with a statement connecting 1 mol of ammonia with the Avogadro Constant.

$$1 \text{ mol of } NH_3 \quad = \quad 6 \cdot 02 \times 10^{23} \text{ molecules of } NH_3$$

As the question refers to **atoms,** this statement is rewritten:

$$1 \text{ mol of } NH_3 \quad = \quad 4 \times 6 \cdot 02 \times 10^{23} \text{ atoms (of N and H)}$$
$$= \quad \mathbf{2 \cdot 408 \times 10^{24} \text{ atoms}}$$

(since 1 molecule of NH_3 contains 4 atoms (1 N and 3 H)

$$\text{So } 0 \cdot 3 \text{ mol of } NH_3 \quad = \quad 0 \cdot 3 \times 2 \cdot 408 \times 10^{24} \text{ atoms}$$
$$= \quad 7 \cdot 224 \times 10^{23} \text{ atoms}$$
$$= \quad \mathbf{7 \cdot 22 \times 10^{23}} \text{ (to 3 significant figures)}$$

WORKED EXAMPLE 5.2

How many electrons are present in 1·2 mol of fluorine gas, F_2?

$$
\begin{aligned}
1 \text{ mol of } F_2 \quad &= \quad 6{\cdot}02 \times 10^{23} \text{ molecules of } F_2 \\
&= \quad 2 \times 6{\cdot}02 \times 10^{23} \text{ atoms of } F \\
&= \quad 1{\cdot}204 \times 10^{24} \text{ atoms of } F \\
&= \quad 9 \times 1{\cdot}204 \times 10^{24} \text{ electrons} \\
&\quad \text{(since each atom contains 9 electrons)} \\
&= \quad 1{\cdot}0836 \times 10^{25} \text{ electrons} \\
1{\cdot}2 \text{ mol of } F_2 \quad &= \quad 1{\cdot}2 \times 1{\cdot}0836 \times 10^{25} \text{ electrons} \\
&= \quad 1{\cdot}30032 \times 10^{25} \\
&= \quad \mathbf{1{\cdot}30 \times 10^{25}} \text{ (to 3 significant figues)}
\end{aligned}
$$

WORKED EXAMPLE 5.3

A sample of methane, CH_4, contains $1{\cdot}204 \times 10^{23}$ hydrogen atoms. How many moles of methane does the sample contain?

$$
\begin{aligned}
1 \text{ mol of } CH_4 \quad &= \quad 6{\cdot}02 \times 10^{23} \text{ molecules of } CH_4 \\
\text{contains} \quad & \quad 4 \times 6{\cdot}02 \times 10^{23} \text{ atoms of } H \\
&= \quad \mathbf{2{\cdot}408 \times 10^{24} \text{ atoms of } H}
\end{aligned}
$$

This statement now connects "mol of CH_4" with "atoms of H". In order to get our answer, in "mol of CH_4", to come out on the right hand side, the statement is reversed:

$$
\begin{aligned}
2{\cdot}408 \times 10^{24} \text{ atoms of H } &\text{ are present in} & 1 & \quad \text{mol of } CH_4 \\[4pt]
1 \text{ atom of H } &\text{ is present in} & \frac{1}{2{\cdot}408 \times 10^{24}} & \quad \text{mol of } CH_4 \\[4pt]
1{\cdot}204 \times 10^{23} \text{ atoms of H } &\text{ are present in} & \frac{1{\cdot}204 \times 10^{23}}{2{\cdot}408 \times 10^{24}} & \quad \text{mol of } CH_4 \\[4pt]
& = & \mathbf{0{\cdot}05} &\ \mathbf{mol\ of\ } \mathbf{CH_4}
\end{aligned}
$$

PROBLEMS 5.1 – 5.20

The problems below are of the type illustrated by Worked Examples 5.1 – 5.3.

5. 1   How many *(a)* molecules and *(b)* atoms are present in 1 mol of hydrogen gas, H_2?

5. 2   How many *(a)* nitrogen atoms and *(b)* hydrogen atoms are present in 1 mol of ammonia, NH_3?

5. 3   How many protons are present in 1 mol of nitrogen gas, N_2?

5. 4   A sample of oxygen gas, O_2, contains $2{\cdot}408 \times 10^{21}$ atoms. How many moles of O_2 are present?

5. 5   How many moles of methane, CH_4, would contain $9{\cdot}03 \times 10^{22}$ hydrogen atoms?

5. 6 How many *(a)* sodium ions and *(b)* oxide ions are present in 0·2 mol of sodium oxide, Na_2O?

5. 7 How many neutrons are present in 0·04 mol of oxygen gas, O_2, containing only the oxygen-18 isotope, i.e. ^{18}O?

5. 8 A sample of neon contains $3·612 \times 10^{23}$ atoms. How many moles of neon does this represent?

5. 9 How many electrons are present in 0·05 mol of ozone, O_3?

5.10 A beaker of dilute sulphuric acid, H_2SO_4, contains $4·816 \times 10^{22}$ hydrogen ions. How many moles of sulphuric acid are present?

5.11 How many protons are present in 1 mole of ethane, C_2H_6?

5.12 A sample of calcium chloride, $CaCl_2$, contains a total of $1·806 \times 10^{20}$ ions. How many moles of calcium chloride are present?

5.13 How many ions are present in 2·25 mol of a solution of dilute sulphuric acid, H_2SO_4?

5.14 A sample of ethane, C_2H_6, contains $2·408 \times 10^{24}$ atoms of carbon. How many moles of ethane are present?

5.15 How many electrons are present in 0·3 mol of methane, CH_4?

5.16 A sample of aluminium nitrate, $Al(NO_3)_3$, contains $6·02 \times 10^{24}$ nitrate ions. How many moles of the aluminium nitrate are present?

5.17 How many protons are present in 2·5 mol of ethanoic acid, CH_3COOH?

5.18 How many ions are present in 0·15 mol of magnesium fluoride, MgF_2?

5.19 A sample of methanoic acid, $HCOOH$, contains $1·204 \times 10^{20}$ electrons. How many moles of the acid are present in the sample?

5.20 How many hydrogen atoms are present in 0·04 mol of propene, C_3H_6?

WORKED EXAMPLE 5.4

How many atoms are present in 1·2 g of magnesium?

The problem here involves **two** meanings of the mole, **mass** and **number**, so we state these meanings below, as applied to Mg.

$$1 \text{ mol of Mg} = 24 \text{ g}$$
$$1 \text{ mol of Mg} = 6{\cdot}02 \times 10^{23} \text{ atoms of Mg}$$

Since these two statements both say "1 mole of Mg = ..." on the left hand side, the two right hand sides must also be the same. We can thus write:

$$24 \text{ g} = 6{\cdot}02 \times 10^{23} \text{ atoms of Mg}$$

OR, expressing this the other way round,

$$6{\cdot}02 \times 10^{23} \text{ atoms of Mg} = 24 \text{ g}$$

Since we want the final answer to come out as a number of atoms on the right hand side, we choose the first of the two forms:

$$24 \text{ g} = 6{\cdot}02 \times 10^{23} \text{ atoms of Mg}$$
$$1 \text{ g} = \frac{6{\cdot}02 \times 10^{23}}{24} \text{ atoms of Mg}$$

$$1{\cdot}2 \text{ g} = \frac{1{\cdot}2 \times 6{\cdot}02 \times 10^{23}}{24} \text{ atoms of Mg}$$
$$= \mathbf{3{\cdot}01 \times 10^{22} \text{ atoms of Mg}}$$

WORKED EXAMPLE 5.5

How many oxygen atoms are present in 0·22 g of carbon dioxide, CO_2?

As before, statements defining the two appropriate definitions of the mole are written.

$$1 \text{ mol of } CO_2 = 44 \text{ g}$$
$$1 \text{ mol of } CO_2 = 6{\cdot}02 \times 10^{23} \text{ molecules of } CO_2$$

The second of these statements requires to be adjusted to suit the question which refers, not to **molecules of CO_2**, but to **atoms of O**. Since each molecule of CO_2 contains 2 atoms of O, we write:

$$1 \text{ mole of } CO_2 \quad \text{contains} \quad 1{\cdot}204 \times 10^{24} \text{ atoms of O}$$

Since this statement and the first one above both refer to "1 mol of CO_2 ..." we can say:

$$44 \text{ g of } CO_2 \quad \text{contains} \quad 1{\cdot}204 \times 10^{24} \quad \text{atoms of O}$$
$$1 \text{ g of } CO_2 \quad \text{contains} \quad \frac{1{\cdot}204 \times 10^{24}}{44} \quad \text{atoms of O}$$

$$0{\cdot}22 \text{ g of } CO_2 \quad \text{contains} \quad \frac{0{\cdot}22 \times 1{\cdot}204 \times 10^{24}}{44} \text{ atoms of O}$$
$$= \mathbf{6{\cdot}02 \times 10^{21} \text{ atoms of O}}$$

WORKED EXAMPLE 5.6

What mass of ammonia, NH_3, would contain $2 \cdot 408 \times 10^{22}$ protons?

1 mol of NH_3	=	17 g
1 mol of NH_3	=	$6 \cdot 02 \times 10^{23}$ molecules of NH_3
	contains	$6 \cdot 02 \times 10^{24}$ protons

(since each atom of N contains 7 protons and each H atom contains 1 proton, so each NH_3 molecule contains 10 protons.)

Connecting the first and the last of these statements, with "g of NH_3" on the right hand side, we have:

$6 \cdot 02 \times 10^{24}$	protons are contained in	17	g of NH_3
1	proton is contained in	$\dfrac{17}{6 \cdot 02 \times 10^{24}}$	g of NH_3
$2 \cdot 408 \times 10^{22}$	protons are contained in	$\dfrac{2 \cdot 408 \times 10^{22} \times 17}{6 \cdot 02 \times 10^{24}}$	g of NH_3
	=	**$0 \cdot 068$ g of NH_3**	

WORKED EXAMPLE 5.7

What is the mass, in grams, of 1 molecule of ammonia?

This problem is actually no different from the previous ones connecting the mass of a substance and a number of particles, although the fact that the number of particles referred to is 1 (molecule of ammonia) is sometimes confusing. We proceed exactly as before.

1 mol of NH_3	=	17 g
1 mol of NH_3	=	$6 \cdot 02 \times 10^{23}$ molecules of NH_3

We require our answer to come out as a mass, in grams on the right hand side, so we connect the above statements as below:

$6 \cdot 02 \times 10^{23}$	molecules of NH_3	=	17	g
1	molecule of NH_3	=	$\dfrac{17}{6 \cdot 02 \times 10^{23}}$	g
		=	**$2 \cdot 82 \times 10^{-23}$ g** (to 3 significant figures)	

PROBLEMS 5.21 — 5.40

These problems are of the type illustrated by Worked Examples 5.4 – 5.7 involving masses and numbers of particles.

5.21 How many atoms are present in 0.2 g of neon?

5.22 What is the mass of 1.505×10^{22} atoms of carbon?

5.23 How many atoms are present in 16.25 g of zinc?

5.24 What is the mass of 4.816×10^{21} atoms of cobalt?

5.25 What is the mass, in grams, of 1 atom of gold?

5.26 How many atoms are present in 7.8 g of potassium?

5.27 What is the mass of 1.204×10^{21} atoms of magnesium?

5.28 How many *(a)* molecules and *(b)* atoms are present in 4 g of hydrogen, H_2?

5.29 What is the mass of 3.01×10^{21} molecules of nitrogen, N_2?

5.30 What is the mass, in grams, of 1 molecule of carbon dioxide, CO_2?

5.31 How many *(a)* molecules and *(b)* atoms are present in 2.64 g of carbon dioxide, CO_2?

5.32 A sample of hydrogen gas, H_2, contains 1.505×10^{21} atoms. What is the mass of the sample?

5.33 How many *(a)* protons and *(b)* neutrons are present in 3.5 g of the isotope ^{14}C?

5.34 A sample of neon contains 3.01×10^{24} protons.
  (a) How many atoms does the sample contain?
  (b) What is the mass of the sample?

5.35 How many *(a)* sodium ions and *(b)* sulphate ions are present in 11.36 g of sodium sulphate, Na_2SO_4?

5.36 What is the mass, in grams, of 1 molecule of ozone, O_3?

5.37 A sample of zinc contains 4.515×10^{19} electrons. What mass is the sample?

5.38 A solution of iron (III) nitrate, $Fe(NO_3)_3$, is made by dissolving 0.968 g of the substance in water. How many nitrate ions are present in the solution?

5.39 How many neutrons are present in 0.84 g of ethene, C_2H_4, which contains only the ^{12}C and ^{1}H isotopes?

5.40 A sample of aluminium oxide, Al_2O_3, contains 1.204×10^{21} oxide ions. What mass is the sample of aluminium oxide?

WORKED EXAMPLE 5.8

A solution of sulphuric acid has 1.204×10^{21} hydrogen ions in 500 cm³ of solution. What is the concentration of the acid solution?

In this type of problem, we need to use the definition of concentration (molarity), measured in mol l^{-1}, which was revised in Chapter 2. We are asked for the concentration and told the number of litres (500 cm³ = 0.5 l). We require to find firstly the number of moles of sulphuric acid present. We start with a true statement about sulphuric acid in terms of numbers of particles.

$$
\begin{aligned}
1 \text{ mol of } H_2SO_4 \quad &= \quad 6.02 \times 10^{23} \text{ molecules } H_2SO_4 \\
\text{contains} \quad &\quad 2 \times 6.02 \times 10^{23} \text{ hydrogen ions} \\
&= \quad 1.204 \times 10^{24} \text{ hydrogen ions}
\end{aligned}
$$

(since each H_2SO_4 molecule produces two hydrogen ions in solution.)

Reversing this last statement to give "mol of H_2SO_4" on the RHS, we have:

1.204×10^{24}	hydrogen ions are contained in	1	mol of H_2SO_4
1	hydrogen ion is contained in	$\dfrac{1}{1.204 \times 10^{24}}$	mol of H_2SO_4
1.204×10^{21}	hydrogen ions are contained in	$\dfrac{1.204 \times 10^{21}}{1.204 \times 10^{24}}$	mol of H_2SO_4
	=	0.001 mol of H_2SO_4	

Having calculated the number of moles of acid, we can put this, and the volume in litres, into the appropriate equation to obtain the concentration:

$$
\begin{aligned}
\text{concentration} \quad &= \quad \frac{\text{number of moles}}{\text{volume (in litres)}} \\
&= \quad \frac{0.001}{0.5} \\
&= \quad \mathbf{0.002 \text{ mol } } l^{-1}
\end{aligned}
$$

PROBLEMS 5.41 — 5.60

These problems relate concentration with numbers of particles in solution, as in Worked Example 5.8.

5.41 How many ions are present in a 200 cm³ solution of 1 mol l^{-1} sodium chloride, NaCl?

5.42 What is the concentration of a 250 cm³ solution of sulphuric acid, H_2SO_4, containing 2.408×10^{23} sulphate ions?

5.43 A 0.2 mol l^{-1} solution of nitric acid, HNO_3, contains 1.204×10^{22} ions. What volume is the solution?

5.44 How many (a) ammonium ions and (b) carbonate ions are present in 100 cm³ of a 0.5 mol l^{-1} solution of ammonium carbonate, $(NH_4)_2CO_3$?

5.45 1.806×10^{22} molecules of pure sulphuric acid, H_2SO_4, are dissolved in water to make 600 cm³ of solution. What is the concentration of the diluted solution?

5.46 3.612×10^{21} ions are present in a 0.25 mol l^{-1} solution of sulphric acid, H_2SO_4. What is the volume of the solution?

5.47 How many (a) ammonium ions and (b) phosphate ions are present in 1.2 litres of a 0.2 mol l^{-1} solution of ammonium phosphate, $(NH_4)_3PO_4$?

5.48 A 400 cm^3 solution of calcium nitrate, $Ca(NO_3)_2$ contains $3 \cdot 01 \times 10^{22}$ nitrate ions. What is the concentration of the salt solution?

5.49 What volume of a 0·5 mol l^{-1} solution of sodium carbonate, Na_2CO_3, would contain $7 \cdot 224 \times 10^{21}$ carbonate ions?

5.50 What is the concentration of a 250 cm^3 solution of iron(III) nitrate, $Fe(NO_3)_3$, in which there are $1 \cdot 806 \times 10^{22}$ nitrate ions?

5.51 $7 \cdot 525 \times 10^{21}$ molecules of hydrogen chloride gas, HCl, are dissolved to make 250 cm^3 of dilute hydrochloric acid solution. What is the concentration of the solution?

5.52 How many ions does 50 cm^3 of a 0·2 mol l^{-1} solution of sodium phosphate, Na_3PO_4, contain?

5.53 $3 \cdot 01 \times 10^{21}$ potassium ions are present in a 0·1 mol l^{-1} solution of potassium carbonate, K_2CO_3. What volume is the solution?

5.54 How many ions are contained in 40 cm^3 of a 0·2 mol l^{-1} solution of sodium nitrate, $NaNO_3$?

5.55 200 cm^3 of dilute sulphuric acid, H_2SO_4, contains $4 \cdot 816 \times 10^{21}$ hydrogen ions. What is the concentration of the acid?

5.56 How many molecules of ethanol, C_2H_5OH, are contained in 30 cm^3 of a 0·4 mol l^{-1} solution of the compound?

5.57 50 cm^3 of a solution of magnesium nitrate, $Mg(NO_3)_2$, contains $9 \cdot 03 \times 10^{20}$ nitrate ions. What is the concentration of the solution?

5.58 A 0·01 mol l^{-1} solution of aluminium nitrate, $Al(NO_3)_3$, contains $1 \cdot 505 \times 10^{20}$ ions. What volume is the solution?

5.59 What is the concentration of a 300 cm^3 solution of sodium hydroxide, NaOH, containing a total of $3 \cdot 612 \times 10^{22}$ ions?

5.60 How many (a) ammonium and (b) sulphate ions are present in 15 cm^3 of a 0·12 mol l^{-1} solution of ammonium sulphate, $(NH_4)_2SO_4$?

WORKED EXAMPLE 5.9

At 273 K and 1 atmosphere pressure, sulphur dioxide, SO_2, has a density of 2·93 g l^{-1}. How many molecules would be present in 25 cm^3 of the gas under these conditions?

This type of problem is really the same as those connecting the mass of a substance with the number of particles present, although it involves the density of a gas. Problems involving gas densities, masses and volumes were considered in Chapter 4; it is important that the work of that chapter is understood before continuing. Note that in Chapter 4, two methods were given for connecting the terms mass, density and volume; Method 1 used equations and Method 2 used "direct variation". In this and the following two Worked Examples, only Method 1 is shown, although Method 2 would be equally suitable.

The mass of gas can be calculated from the density and volume of the gas, once the volume has been converted to litres:

$$\text{mass} \quad = \quad \text{density} \quad \times \quad \text{volume}$$

$$= \quad 2 \cdot 93 \quad \times \quad 0 \cdot 025$$

$$= \quad \mathbf{0 \cdot 007325 \, g}$$

This mass can then be changed into a number of molecules by using the method used earlier in this chapter.

1 mol of SO_2	=	64 g	
1 mol of SO_2	=	$6·02 \times 10^{23}$	molecules

So:

64 g	contains	$6·02 \times 10^{23}$	molecules
1 g	contains	$\dfrac{6·02 \times 10^{23}}{64}$	molecules
0·007325 g	contains	$\dfrac{6·02 \times 10^{23} \times 0·007325}{64}$	molecules
	=	**$6·89 \times 10^{19}$ molecules** (to 3 significant figures)	

WORKED EXAMPLE 5.10

At 298 K and at 1 atmosphere pressure, methane, CH_4, has a density of 0·714 g l^{-1}. A sample of the gas contains $2·408 \times 10^{20}$ molecules. What volume is the sample under these conditions?

1 mol of CH_4	=	16 g	
1 mol of CH_4	=	$6·02 \times 10^{23}$	molecules

So:

$6·02 \times 10^{23}$	molecules have a mass of	16	g
1	molecule has a mass of	$\dfrac{16}{6·02 \times 10^{23}}$	g
$2·408 \times 10^{20}$	molecules have a mass of	$\dfrac{16 \times 2·408 \times 10^{20}}{6·02 \times 10^{23}}$	g
	=	0·0064 g	

Taking this mass and the density value given, we calculate the volume:

$$\text{volume} = \frac{\text{mass}}{\text{density}}$$

$$= \frac{0·0064}{0·714}$$

$$= \textbf{0·00896} \, \boldsymbol{l} \, \textbf{(8·96 cm}^3\textbf{)} \quad \text{(to 3 significant figures)}$$

WORKED EXAMPLE 5.11

A 50 cm^3 sample of a gas with density 1·12 g l^{-1} contains $1·204 \times 10^{21}$ molecules. Calculate the molecular mass of the gas.

We can obtain the mass of this quantity of gas from the density and the volume:

$$\text{mass} = \text{density} \times \text{volume}$$

$$= 1·12 \times 0·05$$

$$= 0·056 \, \text{g}$$

From the number of molecules we can calculate the number of moles of gas present.

$6 \cdot 02 \times 10^{23}$	molecules	=	1	mol of the gas
1	molecule	=	$\dfrac{1}{6 \cdot 02 \times 10^{23}}$	mol of the gas
$1 \cdot 204 \times 10^{21}$	molecules	=	$\dfrac{1 \cdot 204 \times 10^{21}}{6 \cdot 02 \times 10^{23}}$	mol of the gas
		=	$0 \cdot 002$ mol of the gas	

Connecting the **number of moles** of gas in the sample with its **mass**, we can calculate the **mass of 1 mol**.

$0 \cdot 002$	mol of the gas weighs	$0 \cdot 056$	g
1	mol of the gas weighs	$\dfrac{0 \cdot 056}{0 \cdot 002}$	g

$$= \quad \textbf{28 g}$$

So the molecular mass of the gas is 28. Note that the molecular mass has no unit, although the mass of 1 mol is expressed in grams.

PROBLEMS 5.61 — 5.80

These problems are of the type shown in Worked Examples 5.9 – 5.11

5.61 Under certain conditions, carbon dioxide, CO_2, has a density of $1 \cdot 98$ g l^{-1}. How many molecules will be present in 200 cm^3 of the gas under these conditions?

5.62 $7 \cdot 224 \times 10^{20}$ molecules of a gas of molecular mass 34 are contained in a sample of 100 cm^3. Calculate the density of the gas under these conditions.

5.63 At 273 K and 1 atmosphere pressure, carbon monoxide, CO, has a density of $1 \cdot 25$ g l^{-1}. What volume of the gas would contain $4 \cdot 816 \times 10^{20}$ molecules under these conditions?

5.64 A 50 cm^3 sample of a gas contains $1 \cdot 505 \times 10^{21}$ molecules. If its density under these conditions is $1 \cdot 7$ g l^{-1}, calculate its molecular mass.

5.65 A 25 cm^3 sample of xenon under certain conditions contains $1 \cdot 204 \times 10^{20}$ atoms of the gas. Calculate the density of the gas under these conditions.

5.66 How many atoms are in a 60 cm^3 sample of chlorine, Cl_2, under conditions where its density is $2 \cdot 7$ g l^{-1}?

5.67 Fluorine, F_2, has a density of $1 \cdot 9$ g l^{-1} under certain conditions. How many atoms of fluorine would be contained in a 20 cm^3 sample under these conditions?

5.68 Nitrogen, N_2, has a density of $1 \cdot 5$ g l^{-1} under certain conditions. What volume would $3 \cdot 01 \times 10^{21}$ molecules of nitrogen occupy under these conditions?

5.69 200 cm^3 of ammonia, NH_3, contains $9 \cdot 03 \times 10^{21}$ molecules. What is the density of the gas under these conditions?

5.70 How many atoms are present in 150 cm^3 of butane, C_4H_{10}, under conditions where the gas has a density of $2 \cdot 5$ g l^{-1}?

5.71 Under certain conditions, a 150 cm^3 sample of a gas of density $2 \cdot 35$ g l^{-1} contains $4 \cdot 816 \times 10^{21}$ molecules. Calculate its molecular mass.

5.72   Hydrogen, H_2, has a density of $0 \cdot 12$ g l^{-1} under certain conditions of temperature and pressure. How many atoms would be present in a 20 cm^3 sample of the gas?

5.73   Neon has a density of $1 \cdot 1$ g l^{-1} under certain conditions. What volume would $3 \cdot 01 \times 10^{20}$ atoms of the gas occupy under these conditions?

5.74   How many atoms would be contained in 120 cm^3 of carbon dioxide, CO_2, under conditions in which the density of the gas is $2 \cdot 2$ g l^{-1}?

5.75   A diatomic, gaseous element has a density of $1 \cdot 33$ g l^{-1}. Under these conditions, $1 \cdot 505 \times 10^{21}$ molecules of the gas occupy a volume of 60 cm^3. Calculate the molecular mass of the gas and, hence, identify it.

5.76   What volume would $8 \cdot 428 \times 10^{22}$ molecules of sulphur dioxide, SO_2, occupy if the density of the gas under these conditions is $3 \cdot 2$ g l^{-1}?

5.77   75 cm^3 of ethane, C_2H_6, contains $1 \cdot 204 \times 10^{22}$ hydrogen atoms. What is the density of the gas under these conditions?

5.78   Methane, CH_4, has a density of $0 \cdot 65$ g l^{-1} under certain conditions of temperature and pressure. How many hydrogen atoms are present in 45 cm^3 of the gas under these conditions?

5.79 $7 \cdot 224 \times 10^{21}$ atoms in total are present in 80 cm^3 of ammonia, NH_3. Calculate the density of ammonia under these conditions.

5.80   Ethyne, C_2H_2, has a density of $1 \cdot 4$ g l^{-1} under certain conditions of temperature and pressure. How many atoms would be present in 120 cm^3 of the gas under these conditions?

6. ELECTROLYSIS AND THE FARADAY

The quantity of electrical charge, Q, measured in Coulombs (C) flowing in a circuit is related to the current, I, measured in Amperes, "Amps" (A) and the time in seconds (s) by the equation:

$$Q = It$$

It is known experimentally that the quantity of electrical charge on 1 mole of electrons is 96 500 C. This important value is known as the Faraday, symbol F (1 F = 96 500 C).

In an electrolysis, where a metal is deposited or a gas given off at an electrode, we can write the ion-electron equation for the reaction at each electrode. For example, the electrode reactions in the electrolysis of copper(II) sulphate solution are:

$$- \text{electrode} \quad Cu^{2+} \quad + 2e^- \longrightarrow \quad Cu$$
$$+ \text{electrode} \quad 2H_2O \longrightarrow \quad O_2 \quad + \quad 4H^+ \quad + \quad 4e^-$$

These ion-electron equations are important because they tell us that:

> 1 mol of copper is deposited by the passage of 2 mol of electrons

and

> 1 mol of oxygen gas (O_2) is given off by the passage of 4 mol of electrons.

Thus, if we know the quantity of charge which has passed (from the current and the time), we can calculate the number of moles of electrons passed and hence the number of moles of substance produced at an electrode. From this, we can obtain the mass of substance.

The application of this theory is better seen by studying the worked examples and problems that follow.

WORKED EXAMPLE 6.1

What mass of nickel is deposited in the electrolysis of nickel(II) sulphate solution if a current of 0·4 A is passed for 120 minutes?

The total charge passed is calculated:

$$Q \quad = \quad I \times t$$
$$= \quad 0\cdot4 \times 120 \times 60 \quad \text{(Note: time is in seconds.)}$$
$$= \quad \textbf{2880 C}$$

We then calculate the number of moles of electrons that this charge represents:

965 000 C	is the charge on	1	mol of electrons
1 C	is the charge on	$\dfrac{1}{96\,500}$	mol of electrons
2880 C	is the charge on	$\dfrac{2880}{96\,500}$	mol of electrons
	=	**0·02984**	**mol of electrons** (rounded)

We now write the ion-electron equation to relate the number of moles of electrons with the number of moles of nickel deposited. The compound being electrolysed is nickel(II) sulphate, so the nickel ion present is Ni^{2+} and the equation for the deposition of Ni metal must be:

$$Ni^{2+} \quad + \quad 2e^- \longrightarrow \quad Ni$$

This equation tells us that:

2	mol of electrons deposits	1	mol of Ni
1	mol of electrons deposits	0·5	mol of Ni
0·02984	mol of electrons deposits	0·02984 × 0·5	mol of Ni

$$= \textbf{0·01492 mol of Ni}$$

The number of moles of nickel deposited have been calculated, but the problem asks for the mass of nickel. This is the final part of the calculation.

1	mol of Ni	=	59 g
0·01492	mol of Ni	=	0·01492 × 59 g
		=	**0·880 g** (rounded to 3 significant figures)

PROBLEMS 6.1 – 6.15

The problems below are of the type illustrated by Worked Example 6.1. Although the last few problems involve large electrical currents used in industrial electrolyses, and the masses of product are expressed in kg in the answers, the same method should be used as for the earlier "laboratory scale" problems.

In the problems in this chapter, ion-electron equations are only given where they may be unfamiliar. Where a metal is being deposited, the equation can be readily worked out from the charge on the metal ion.

6.1   In the electrolysis of copper(II) sulphate solution, a current of 0·1 A flowed for 60 minutes. Calculate the mass of copper which is deposited at the negative electrode.

6.2   In the electrolysis of a molten tin(IV) compound, a current of 0·2 A flowed for 15 minutes. Calculate the mass of tin deposited.

6.3   In the electrolysis of silver(I) nitrate solution, a current of 0·15 A flowed for 30 minutes. Calculate the mass of silver deposited.

6.4   A dilute solution of sulphuric acid is electrolysed by passing a current of 0·25 A through it for 20 minutes. The ion-electron equation for the reaction taking place at the negative electrode is:

$$2H^+ + 2e^- \longrightarrow H_2$$

Calculate the mass of hydrogen gas given off at this electrode during the electrolysis.

6.5   Molten lead(II) bromide is electrolysed using a current of 0·4 A for two hours. Calculate the mass of *(a)* lead and *(b)* bromine produced at the negative and positive electrodes respectively. The equation for the reaction at the positive electrode is:

$$2Br^- \longrightarrow Br_2 + 2e^-$$

6.6   The electrode reactions taking place in the electrolysis of sodium hydroxide solution are:

$$\text{positive electrode:} \quad 4OH^- \longrightarrow 2H_2O + O_2 + 4e^-$$
$$\text{negative electrode:} \quad 2H_2O + 2e^- \longrightarrow H_2 + 2OH^-$$

Sodium hydroxide solution is electrolysed using a current of 0·15 A for 30 minutes. Calculate the mass of *(a)* hydrogen and *(b)* oxygen evolved at the electrodes.

6. 7 In the electrolysis of molten aluminium oxide, a current of 0·25 A flowed for two hours. Calculate the mass of aluminium deposited.

6. 8 In the electrolysis of dilute nitric acid, the electrode reactions are:

positive electrode: $2H_2O \longrightarrow O_2 + 4H^+ + 4e^-$
negative electrode: $2H^+ + 2e^- \longrightarrow H_2$

Dilute nitric acid is electrolysed using a current of 0·15 A for 40 minutes. Calculate the mass of *(a)* hydrogen and *(b)* oxygen evolved.

6. 9 Copper is purified by electrolysing copper(II) sulphate solution with a positive electrode of impure copper and a negative electrode of pure copper. As the electrolysis takes place, the impure copper dissolves in the solution and pure copper is deposited on the negative electrode. If a current of 50 A was passed for ten hours in such an electrolysis, what mass of pure copper would be deposited?

6.10 In the industrial manufacture of aluminium, molten aluminium oxide is electrolysed using a current of 10^5 A. Calculate the mass, in kg, of aluminium produced in a period of 24 hours by this process.

6.11 Sodium is manufactured by the electrolysis of molten sodium chloride using a current of $2·5 \times 10^4$ A. Calculate the mass, in kg, of sodium produced in a two hour period.

6.12 A current of 500 A is used to nickel plate metal objects by the electrolysis of a solution of a nickel(II) salt. Calculate the mass, in kg, of nickel which would be deposited every 24 hours by this process.

6.13 Magnesium is produced electrolytically using a current of 2×10^5 A through a molten magnesium compound. What mass of magnesium, in kg, would be produced during an eight hour period by this process?

6.14 Chromium can be plated on metal objects by the electrolysis of a chromium(III) solution. What mass of chromium would be plated on the objects if a current of 2×10^3 A were applied for one hour?

6.15 An electrolytic smelter uses a current of $1·4 \times 10^5$ A to obtain aluminium from its molten oxide. What mass of aluminium, in kg, would be produced in eight hours of this smelter's operation?

WORKED EXAMPLE 6.2

For how long, in minutes, must a current of 0·25 A flow in the electrolysis of molten aluminium oxide to cause the deposition of 1·08 g of aluminium at the negative electrode?

In this type of example, instead of being told current and time, we have to calculate one of these quantities, having been given information about the amount of product at an electrode. We start by calculating how many moles of aluminium have been deposited.

$$27 \text{ g} = 1 \text{ mol of Al}$$
$$1 \text{ g} = \frac{1}{27} \text{ mol of Al}$$
$$1·08 \text{ g} = \frac{1·08}{27} \text{ mol of Al}$$
$$= \mathbf{0·04} \text{ mol of Al}$$

We next have to find out how many moles of electrons must have been involved. The ion-electron equation for the electrode reaction must be written:

$$Al^{3+} + 3e^- \longrightarrow Al$$

This equation tells us that:

1	mol of Al is deposited by	3 mol of electrons
0·04	mol of Al is deposited by	0·04 × 3 mol of electrons
		= **0·12 mol of electrons**

We now find what quantity of charge this represents:

1	mol of electrons	=	a charge of	96 500 C
0·12	mol of electrons	=	a charge of	0·12 × 96 500 C
			=	**11 580 C**

Since we know that the total charge, current and time are connected by the equation $Q = I \times t$, we can now use the total charge (calculated above) and the known current to calculate the time.

$$Q = I \times t$$
$$11\,580 = 0·25 \times t$$
$$\text{So } t = \frac{11\,580}{0·25} \text{ s}$$
$$= 46\,320 \text{ s}$$
$$= \textbf{772 minutes}$$

PROBLEMS 6.16 — 6.30

Problems 6.16 – 6.30 below are of the type illustrated by Worked Example 6.2.

6.16 6·4 g of copper was deposited at the negative electrode in the electrolysis of copper(II) sulphate solution using a current of 0·5 A. For how long, in minutes, had the current been flowing?

6.17 A solution of sodium fluoride was electrolysed for 20 minutes during which 0·04 g of oxygen was evolved at the positive electrode according to the equation:

$$2H_2O \longrightarrow O_2 + 4H^+ + 4e^-$$

What current must have been flowing?

6.18 In the electrolysis of silver(I) nitrate solution, 1·08 g of silver was deposited in 1 hour. What current must have been flowing?

6.19 When potassium hydroxide solution is electrolysed, the equation for the reaction at the negative electrode is:

$$2H_2O + 2e^- \longrightarrow H_2 + 2OH^-$$

A solution of potassium hydroxide was electrolysed using a current of 0·2 A. If 0·06 g of hydrogen was evolved, for how long, in minutes, had the current been flowing?

6.20 0·32 g of copper was deposited in the electrolysis of a solution of copper(II) nitrate. For how long, in minutes, must the current of 0·5 A have been flowing?

6.21 A solution of nickel(II) sulphate was electrolysed for 20 minutes, during which time 1·18 g of nickel was deposited. What current must have been flowing?

6.22 Copper(II) sulphate solution is electrolysed for 30 minutes, during which time 0·24 g of oxygen is evolved. The equation for this electrode reaction is:

$$2H_2O \longrightarrow O_2 + 4H^+ + 4e^-$$

Calculate the current which had been flowing in the circuit.

6.23 Nickel(II) nitrate solution is electrolysed using a current of 0·15 A, yielding 0·472 g of nickel. For how long, in minutes, had the current been flowing?

6.24 A solution of chromium(III) sulphate is electrolysed for 1 hour, during which 0·312 g of chromium is deposited. What current must have been flowing?

6.25 When dilute sulphuric acid is electrolysed, the evolution of oxygen at the positive electrode is described by the following ion-electron equation:

$$2H_2O \longrightarrow O_2 + 4H^+ + 4e^-$$

Dilute sulphuric acid is electrolysed using a current of 0·12 A. If 0·48 g of oxygen is evolved, for how long, in minutes, must the current have been flowing?

6.26 In the industrial electrolysis of a nickel(II) solution to nickel plate metal objects, a current of 482·5 A was used to deposit 5·31 kg of nickel. How long, in hours, had the electrolysis been running?

6.27 4·16 kg of chromium was plated during three hours of electrolysis of a chromium(III) compound. What current must have been used?

6.28 For how long, in minutes, must a current of $1·2 \times 10^5$ A be applied to obtain 100 kg of aluminium in the industrial electrolysis of aluminium oxide?

6.29 154 kg of sodium was obtained in 10 hours of electrolysis of a molten sodium salt. What current must have been flowing during this time?

6.30 1·84 kg of copper was deposited during four hours of electrolytic purification of copper using a solution of copper(II) sulphate. What current must have been applied?

WORKED EXAMPLE 6.3

In the electrolysis of copper(II) sulphate solution, 0·32 g of copper is deposited at the negative electrode. What mass of oxygen would be evolved at the positive electrode? The electrode reactions are:

$$\text{positive electrode} \quad 2H_2O \longrightarrow O_2 + 4H^+ + 4e^-$$

$$\text{negative electrode} \quad Cu^{2+} + 2e^- \longrightarrow Cu$$

In this type of problem, we are not given any information about current or time; we are given information about the mass of a product at one electrode and asked about the mass of product at the other.

We start by calculating the number of moles of the known product, in this case copper:

$$64 \text{ g of Cu} = 1 \text{ mol of Cu}$$

$$1 \text{ g of Cu} = \frac{1}{64} \text{ mol of Cu}$$

$$0\cdot32 \text{ g of Cu} = \frac{0\cdot32}{64} \text{ mol of Cu}$$

$$= \mathbf{0\cdot005} \text{ mol of Cu}$$

In order to relate this to the mass of product at the other electrode, we first calculate the number of moles of electrons which must have flowed to produce this mass of copper by writing the ion-electron equation:

$$Cu^{2+} + 2e^- \longrightarrow Cu$$

This equation tells us that:

$$1 \text{ mol of Cu is produced by } 2 \text{ mol of electrons}$$

$$0\cdot005 \text{ mol of Cu is produced by } 0\cdot005 \times 2 \text{ mol of electrons}$$

$$= \mathbf{0\cdot01 \text{ mol of electrons}}$$

We then use this figure and the ion-electron equation for the other electrode reaction to obtain the number of moles of oxygen:

$$2H_2O \longrightarrow O_2 + 4H^+ + 4e^-$$

$$4 \text{ mol of electrons produces } 1 \text{ mol of } O_2$$

$$1 \text{ mol of electrons produces } \frac{1}{4} \text{ mol of } O_2$$

$$0\cdot01 \text{ mol of electrons produces } \frac{0\cdot01}{4} \text{ mol of } O_2$$

$$= \mathbf{0\cdot0025 \text{ mol of } O_2}$$

The final part is to change this to a mass of oxygen:

$$1 \text{ mol of } O_2 = 32 \text{ g}$$

$$0\cdot0025 \text{ mol of } O_2 = 0\cdot0025 \times 32 \text{ g}$$

$$= \mathbf{0\cdot08 \text{ g}}$$

PROBLEMS 6.31 – 6.40

These problems are of the type illustrated by Worked Example 6.3.

6.31 In the electrolysis of nickel(II) sulphate solution, 0·04 g of oxygen gas is evolved at the positive electrode according to the equation:

$$2H_2O \longrightarrow O_2 + 4H^+ + 4e^-$$

What mass of nickel would have been deposited at the negative electrode during this process?

6.32 When dilute sulphuric acid is electrolysed, 0·04 g of hydrogen gas is evolved at the negative electrode. What mass of oxygen would be given off at the positive electrode? The electrode reactions are:

negative electrode $\quad 2H^+ + 2e^- \longrightarrow H_2$

positive electrode $\quad 2H_2O \longrightarrow O_2 + 4H^+ + 4e^-$

6.33 When molten calcium chloride is electrolysed, 17·75 g of chlorine is given off at the positive electrode. What mass of calcium would be obtained at the negative electrode? The equation for the reaction taking place at the positive electrode is given below:

$$2Cl^- \longrightarrow Cl_2 + 2e^-$$

6.34 Copper(II) sulphate solution is electrolysed, during which 0·8 g of copper is deposited at the negative electrode. Calculate the mass of oxygen gas which would be evolved at the positive electrode. The equation for the reaction at the positive electrode is:

$$2H_2O \longrightarrow O_2 + 4H^+ + 4e^-$$

6.35 In the electrolysis of nickel(II) nitrate solution, 0·64 g of oxygen is given off at the positive electrode according to the equation below:

$$2H_2O \longrightarrow O_2 + 4H^+ + 4e^-$$

What mass of nickel would have been deposited at the negative electrode?

6.36 Chromium(III) nitrate solution is electrolysed, during which 1·92 g of oxygen is given off at the positive electrode according to the ion-electron equation below:

$$2H_2O \longrightarrow O_2 + 4H^+ + 4e^-$$

What mass of chromium would be obtained at the negative electrode?

6.37 Molten gold(III) bromide is electrolysed, during which 2·4 g of bromine gas is evolved, according to the equation:

$$2Br^- \longrightarrow Br_2 + 2e^-$$

Calculate the mass of gold deposited.

6.38 Two electrolysis cells are set up in series, so that the current flows through one cell and then the other. The first cell contains a molten chromium(III) compound, the other a solution of copper(II) nitrate. If 0·416 g of chromium is deposited in the first cell, calculate the mass of copper produced in the second cell.

6.39 The same quantity of electricity is passed through two solutions, one containing sodium hydroxide solution, the other containing gold(III) nitrate solution. If 3·94 g of gold is deposited from the second solution, calculate the mass of hydrogen produced at the negative electrode in the first cell. The equation for this latter electrode reaction is:

$$2H_2O + 2e^- \longrightarrow H_2 + 2OH^-$$

6.40 The same quantity of electrical charge is passed through two electrolysis cells containing, respectively, dilute sulphuric acid and silver(I) nitrate solution. 0·005 g of hydrogen is evolved at the negative electrode in the first solution, according to the equation:

$$2H^+ + 2e^- \longrightarrow H_2$$

Calculate the mass of silver produced at the negative electrode in the second cell.

WORKED EXAMPLE 6.4

A molten iron salt is electrolysed using a current of 4·74 A for 30 minutes during which 1·65 g of iron is deposited. Calculate the number of positive charges on each iron ion.

In this type of problem we do not know whether the compound is an iron(II) or iron(III) salt which is being electrolysed; that is, we do not know whether it is Fe^{2+} or Fe^{3+} ions which are being discharged. We therefore cannot write the ion-electron equation as we have before. We need to work out the ion-electron equation by calculating the number of moles of electrons which have been passed and then the number of moles of iron which have been deposited.

$$
\begin{aligned}
Q &= It \\
&= 4\cdot74 \times 30 \times 60 \text{ C} \\
&= \mathbf{8532 \text{ C}}
\end{aligned}
$$

$$
\begin{aligned}
96\,500 \text{ C} &= 1 && \text{mol of electrons} \\
1 \text{ C} &= \frac{1}{96\,500} && \text{mol of electrons} \\
8532 \text{ C} &= \frac{8532}{96\,500} && \text{mol of electrons} \\
&= \mathbf{0\cdot0884 \text{ mol of electrons}}
\end{aligned}
$$

$$
\begin{aligned}
56 \text{ g} &= 1 && \text{mol of iron} \\
1 \text{ g} &= \frac{1}{56} && \text{mol of iron} \\
1\cdot65 \text{ g} &= \frac{1\cdot65}{56} && \text{mol of iron} \\
&= \mathbf{0\cdot0295 \text{ mol of iron}}
\end{aligned}
$$

What we have now calculated is that:

    0·0295 mol of Fe was deposited by   0·0884 mol of electrons

So

    1 mol of Fe would be deposited by $\dfrac{0\cdot0884}{0\cdot0295}$ mol of electrons

$$= \mathbf{3 \text{ mol of electrons}} \text{ (rounded)}$$

Thus the charge on the iron ion must be 3+ and the ion-electron equation is:

$$Fe^{3+} + 3e^- \longrightarrow Fe$$

Note that the figures will not always turn out to be exact whole number multiples since the data are usually obtained by experiment and there will be some error as a result. Also, any "rounding" taking place during calculation may contribute to a difference between the calculated relationship and the exact whole-number ratio that we are looking for.

PROBLEMS 6.41 – 6.45

Problems 6.41 – 6.45 are of the type illustrated in Worked Example 6.4

6.41 A solution of a metal nitrate is electrolysed using a current of 0·2 A for one hour, during which 0·328 g of the metal, relative atomic mass 88, is deposited at the negative electrode. Calculate the number of charges on each metal ion.

6.42 A chromium compound was electrolysed using a current of 0·2 A for 45 minutes, during which 0·097 g of chromium was deposited. What was the charge on a chromium ion in this compound?

6.43 A molten vanadium compound is electrolysed using a current of 0·15 A for 40 minutes, during which 0·0634 g of vanadium was deposited. Calculate the charge on the vanadium ions in this compound.

6.44 0·303 g of a metal X, relative atomic mass 39, was obtained from the electrolysis of molten X chloride after a current of 0·25 A had been flowing for 50 minutes. Calculate the charge on the ions of metal X.

6.45 A tin compound is electrolysed using a current of 0·4 A for one hour, during which 0·888 g of tin is deposited. Calculate the charge on each tin ion in the compound.

7. RATE OF REACTION GRAPHS

It has always been of interest to chemists to be able to measure the rate (speed) of chemical reactions. In this chapter we consider two ways of interpreting graphical information about reaction rates. In Part 1, information about the mass, concentration or volume of a substance during a reaction is plotted against time. The resulting curve shows the progress of the reaction; from the gradient (slope) of the graph we can obtain a measure of the average rate of reaction over any time interval. In Part 2, "clock reactions" are introduced; when two reactant solutions are mixed, nothing appears to happen for some time and then, suddenly, a colour change takes place. Such reactions are very useful in studying the rates of reactions, but a different method of analysis is used. In these reactions the reciprocal of the time taken for the colour change (1/t) is used as a measure of the rate of the reaction.

PART 1

The progress of a chemical reaction can be followed by measuring a change in the quantity or concentration of a substance at various times as the reaction takes place. For example, in a reaction where a gas is given off, we could record the loss of mass due to escaping gas using a balance or measure the volume of gas produced with a gas syringe or other device. The sort of apparatus used is shown below.

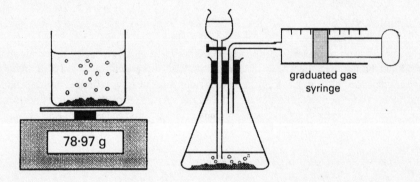

The graphs which would be obtained from these two experiments would be similar to those below.

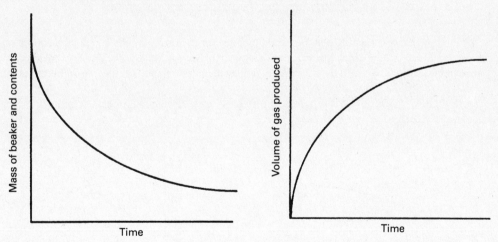

The former graph shows the mass of the beaker and contents dropping as time goes on; the latter graph shows the volume of gas being collected increasing with time. Both graphs start off with a steep gradient (slope), showing a fast reaction at first. As time goes on, the gradients get less steep as the reaction slows down (because the reactants are being used up). Eventually, the gradients reach a point where the graphs become level; that is where the gradient is zero. At this point, no more gas is being produced; in the examples considered, we can say that the reaction has stopped.

We could similarly measure the change in concentration of a reactant or product during a reaction. This might be done by using an electronic meter, such as a pH meter which gives a measure of the concentration of acid or alkali. Another method is to extract small samples of reaction mixture at different times and analyse them, for example by titration. The precise method for following any particular reaction depends on the nature of the reagents involved. The graphs obtained would look like those below.

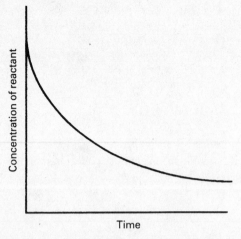

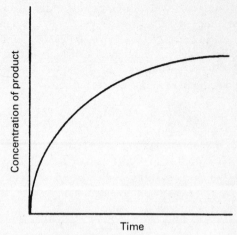

As in the previous examples, both graphs show a fast initial rate of reaction, represented by the steep slope of the graphs at the start. As time goes on, the graphs level off as the reaction slows down. Note that in the first of the two graphs, the concentration of reactant does not necessarily drop to zero, although it will eventually reach a constant value. It might be the case that the reactant being measured was in **excess**; that is, there was more of it than would completely react. Alternatively, while reactants are changing into products, **a back reaction**, in which products change into reactants, may be occurring. When these two reactions take place at the same rate, an **equilibrium** is established. For this reason, we cannot necessarily say that the reaction has "stopped"; we *can* conclude that the **overall** rate of reactants being used up (or products being produced) has reached zero.

We can obtain a numerical value for the rate of reaction over any period of time from a graph such as those shown, using the formula below:

$$\text{rate} \quad = \quad \frac{\text{change in mass } \textbf{or} \text{ volume of gas } \textbf{or} \text{ concentration}}{\text{time interval over which change took place}}$$

Before seeing how this works in practice, it is important to consider the **units** in which rate of reaction may be measured. The unit of rate is simply the unit in which the quantity of substance was measured, **divided by** the unit of time used. Using the currently accepted notation, "divided by seconds" is represented as s^{-1}, and "divided by minutes" is min^{-1}.

Consider the graphs below which show the progress of different reactions against time. The unit for the rate of reaction is noted below the graph in each case.

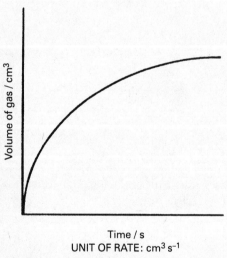

Time / s
UNIT OF RATE: $cm^3\,s^{-1}$

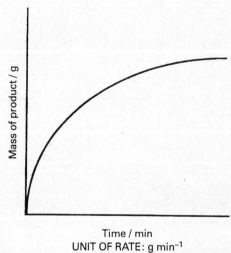

Time / min
UNIT OF RATE: $g\,min^{-1}$

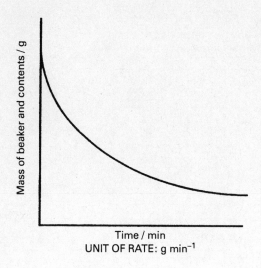

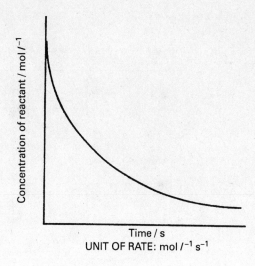

The calculation of rate of reaction from graphs such as those above is now considered in the following Worked Examples.

WORKED EXAMPLE 7.1

The graph below shows the mass of carbon dioxide given off in a chemical reaction, against time.

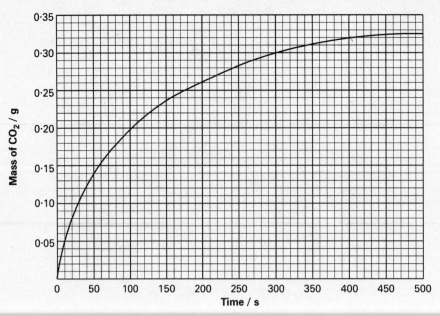

Calculate

(a) **the average rate of reaction over the first 300 s;**

(b) **the average rate of reaction between 200 s and 400 s.**

(a) The rate of reaction is defined in this case by:

$$\text{rate} = \frac{\text{change in mass}}{\text{time interval}}$$

At time = 0 s, mass = 0 g.
At time = 300 s, mass = 0·30 g.

So: rate $= \dfrac{0·30 - 0}{300 - 0} = \dfrac{0·30}{300}$

$= \textbf{0·001 g s}^{-1} \ (\textbf{1} \times \textbf{10}^{-3} \ \textbf{g s}^{-1})$

(b) At time = 200 s, mass = 0·26 g.
At time = 400 s, mass = 0·32 g.

So: rate $= \dfrac{0·32 - 0·26}{400 - 200} = \dfrac{0·06}{200}$

$= \textbf{0·0003 g s}^{-1} \ (\textbf{3} \times \textbf{10}^{-4} \ \textbf{g s}^{-1})$

WORKED EXAMPLE 7.2

The graph below shows the change in concentration of acid against time as a chemical reaction progresses.

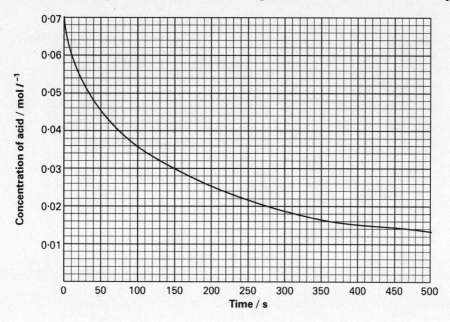

Calculate:

(a) **the average rate of reaction in the first 100 s;**

(b) **the average rate of reaction between 150 s and 350 s.**

(a) The rate of reaction is defined in this case by:

$$\text{rate} = \frac{\text{change in concentration}}{\text{time interval}}$$

At time = 0 s, concentration = 0·07 mol l^{-1}.
At time = 100 s, concentration = 0·036 mol l^{-1}.

So: $$\text{rate} = \frac{0·07 - 0·036}{100 - 0} = \frac{0·034}{100}$$

$$= \textbf{0·00034 mol } \textbf{\textit{l}}^{-1}\textbf{ s}^{-1} \ \ (\textbf{3.4} \times \textbf{10}^{-4}\textbf{ mol } \textbf{\textit{l}}^{-1}\textbf{ s}^{-1})$$

NOTE: The value for "change in concentration" was obtained by taking the smaller concentration from the larger to give a **positive** value. Although in mathematics, the graph shown has a negative **gradient**, a negative **rate of reaction** has no meaning. Always subtract smaller values from larger ones to obtain a positive value for the rate, even when the graph has a downward (negative) gradient.

(b) The answer to the second part of the question is similarly calculated:

At time = 150 s, concentration = 0·03 mol l^{-1}.
At time = 350 s, concentration = 0·016 mol l^{-1}.

So: $$\text{rate} = \frac{0·03 - 0·016}{350 - 150} = \frac{0·014}{200}$$

$$= \textbf{0.00007 mol } \textbf{\textit{l}}^{-1}\textbf{ s}^{-1} \ \ (\textbf{7} \times \textbf{10}^{-5}\textbf{ mol } \textbf{\textit{l}}^{-1}\textbf{ s}^{-1})$$

PROBLEMS 7.1 – 7.10

Problems 7.1 – 7.10 are of the type shown in Worked Examples 7.1 and 7.2.

7.1 The graph below shows the mass of carbon dioxide given off against time in a chemical reaction.

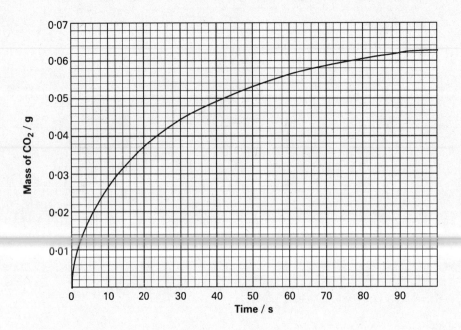

(a) Calculate the average rate of reaction during the first 50 s.

(b) Calculate the average rate of reaction between 30 s and 90 s.

7.2   The graph below shows the change in concentration of a reactant against time during a chemical reaction.

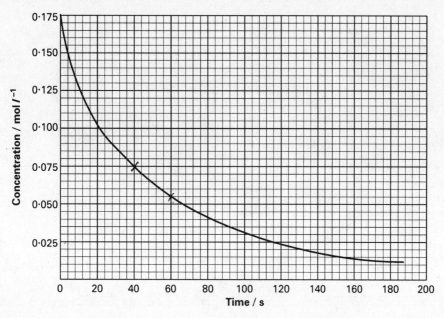

(a)   Calculate the average rate of reaction in the first 100 s of the reaction.

(b)   Calculate the average rate of reaction between 40 s and 60 s.

7.3   The graph below shows how the volume of hydrogen produced in a chemical reaction varies with time.

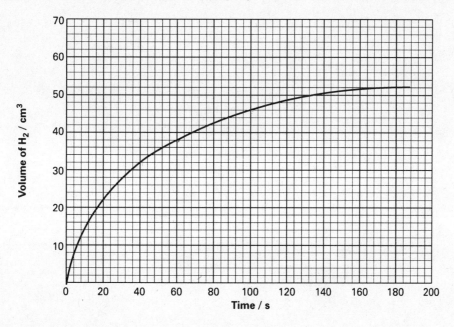

(a)   Calculate the average rate of reaction in the first 40 s.

(b)   Calculate the average rate of reaction between 60 s and 100 s.

7.4 The graph below shows the change in concentration of a reactant, with time, during the progress of a chemical reaction.

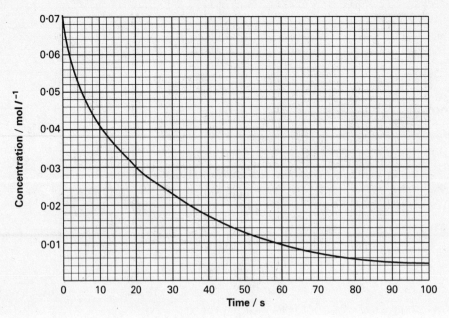

(a) ~~Calculate the average rate of reaction over the first 20 s.~~

(b) Calculate the average rate of reaction between 8 s and 58 s.

7.5 The graph below shows how the mass of carbon dioxide given off during a chemical reaction varies with time.

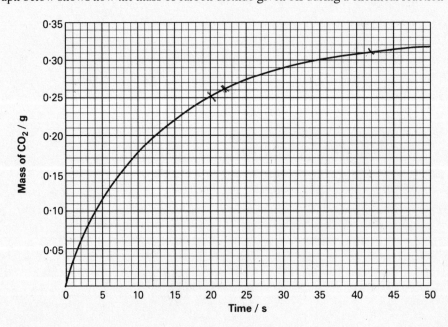

(a) Calculate the average rate of reaction during the first 20 s.

(b) Calculate the average rate of reaction between 22 s and 42 s.

7.6 The graph below shows how the volume of carbon dioxide produced during a chemical reaction varies with time.

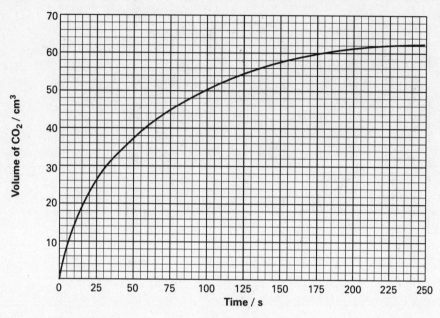

(a) Calculate the average rate of reaction over the first 100 s.

(b) Calculate the average rate of reaction between 125 s and 175 s.

7.7 The graph below shows how the concentration of acid changes during the progress of a chemical reaction.

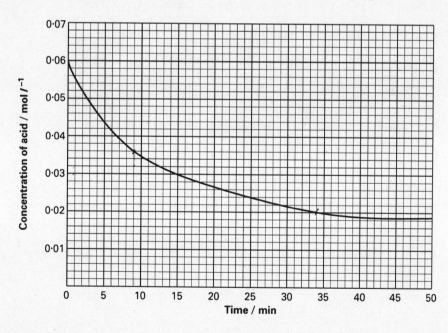

(a) Calculate the average rate of reaction during the first 15 min of the reaction.

(b) Calculate the average rate of reaction between 9 min and 34 min.

7.8 The graph below shows how the mass of a beaker and its contents change as a gas is given off during the course of a chemical reaction.

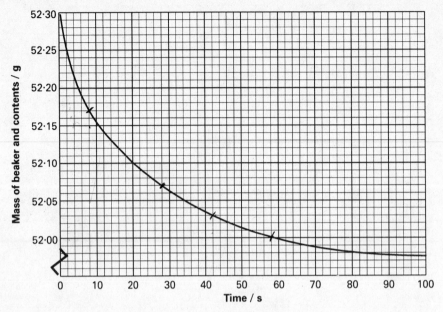

(a) Calculate the average rate of reaction between 8 s and 28 s.

(b) Calculate the average rate of reaction between 42 s and 58 s.

7.9 The graph below shows how the volume of gas produced changes during a chemical reaction.

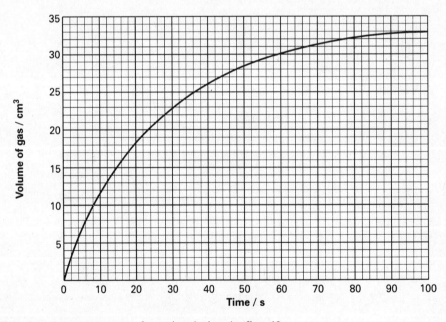

(a) Calculate the average rate of reaction during the first 60 s.

(b) Calculate the average rate of reaction between 40 s and 80 s.

7.10 The graph below shows how the concentration of a reactant changes during the chemical reaction.

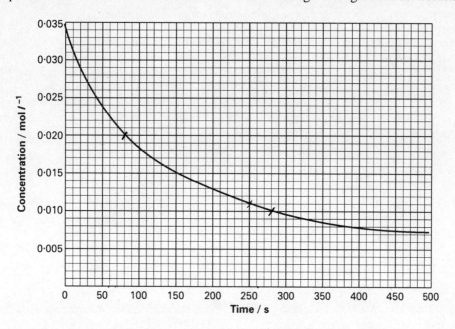

(a) Calculate the average rate of reaction during the first 250 s.

(b) Calculate the average rate of reaction between 80 s and 280 s.

PART 2

In this part of the chapter we consider the interpretation of graphs obtained from "clock reaction" data. A clock reaction is so called because, when two solutions containing the reactants are mixed, nothing appears to happen for some time and then a quick colour change takes place.

A common example of a clock reaction is that between hydrochloric acid and the thiosulphate ion, $S_2O_3^{2-}$. Some time after the two solutions are mixed, a cloudiness of tiny particles of sulphur appears. In rate of reaction studies, it is usual to place a piece of paper with a pencil cross drawn on it under the beaker in which the solutions are mixed. The time taken for the cross to disappear completely is measured for the same reaction, but under different conditions of concentration, temperature, etc.

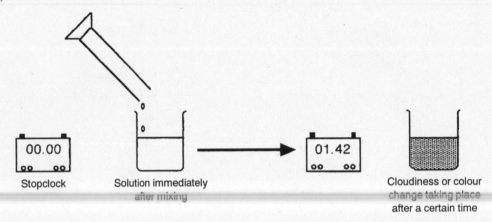

Stopclock Solution immediately after mixing Cloudiness or colour change taking place after a certain time

The time taken for a colour change, or a cross to disappear, is an easy quantity to measure and this is what makes clock reactions so handy for studying the factors affecting reaction rates. However, the time taken is not **directly** a measure of the rate of reaction. A moment's thought tells us that the **longer the time taken** for the colour change, the **slower** the reaction. And, of course, the **shorter the time taken** the **faster** the reaction. The relationship between the time taken and the rate of reaction is known in mathematics as **inverse proportion** (or **variation**). This simply means that, as one quantity increases, the other quantity decreases.

We can turn our "time taken" (t) measurement into a value which gives a measure of rate of reaction simply by taking its **reciprocal** ($1/t$). That is:

$$\text{rate of reaction} \quad = \quad \frac{1}{t}$$

To illustrate this, consider the table below containing the simplified results from a series of experiments in which increasing concentrations of a solution were used in a clock reaction, all other factors being kept constant.

Concentration (arbitrary units)	Time taken $t\,/\,s$	Rate $\frac{1}{t}\,/\,s^{-1}$
1	50	0·02
2	25	0·04
3	16·7	0·06
4	12·5	0·08
5	10	0·10

As might be expected, the time taken for the colour change gets shorter as the concentration is increased in each successive experiment from 1 unit to 5 units. That is, the reaction gets faster as we increase the concentration. The right hand column, entitled "RATE", has $1/t$ calculated for each of the values for t. It can be seen that **these** values go up in line with the increasing concentration; that is, they give a value which is proportional to the rate of reaction.

Before going on to consider graphs of such data, some points need to be noted.

■ Firstly, since the unit of "time taken" will be s or min, the unit of rate, obtained by calculating $1/t$, will be s^{-1} or min^{-1}.

■ Secondly, if rate is obtained by taking $1/t$, t can be obtained by calculating 1/rate. If this is not immediately obvious, practise converting time to rate and rate to time using the figures in the table. (But note that the figures for concentration = 3 units involved rounding in the calculation of rate.)

■ Lastly, most scientific calculators have a button, usually labelled "$1/x$", which will carry out the reciprocal calculation directly; if not already familiar with its use, it is worth getting practice using it in the examples in this part of the chapter.

Rate of reaction studies involving clock reaction data usually involve carrying experiments out using different concentrations of solutions or at different temperatures. The Worked Examples following illustrate these two situations, although the method used for interpreting the graphs is the same in each case.

WORKED EXAMPLE 7.3

The graph below shows the rate of a clock reaction against concentration of solution. The rate is expressed as the reciprocal of the time taken for cloudiness to appear.

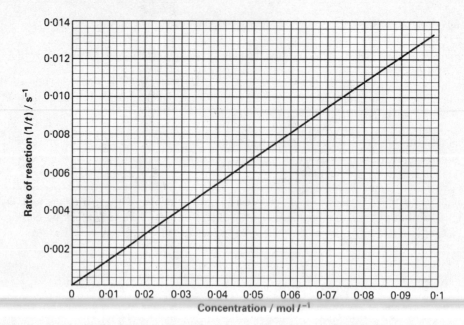

(a) How long did the cloudiness take to appear when the concentration was 0·03 mol l^{-1}?

(b) At what concentration did the cloudiness take 100 s to appear?

(a) From the graph, at a concentration of 0·03 mol l^{-1}, the rate of reaction is 0·004 s^{-1}. The time taken is the **reciprocal** of the rate; that is:

$$\text{time taken} \quad = \quad \frac{1}{0·004}$$

$$= \quad \textbf{250 s}$$

(b) The rate of reaction is the **reciprocal** of the time taken for reaction; that is, when the time taken is 100 s, the rate of reaction is given by:

$$\text{rate} \quad = \quad \frac{1}{100}$$

$$= \quad \textbf{0·01 } \textbf{s}^{-1}$$

From the graph, this value for the rate of reaction occurs at a concentration of **0·074 mol l^{-1}**.

WORKED EXAMPLE 7.4

The graph below shows how the rate of a clock reaction varies with the temperature at which it is carried out. The rate is expressed as the reciprocal of the time taken for a colour change to appear.

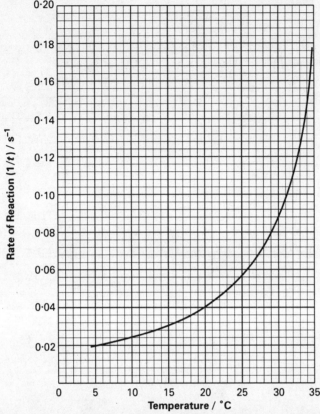

(a) After how long did the colour change take place when the reaction was carried out at 29 °C?

(b) At what temperature would the colour change have taken 25 s to occur?

(a) From the graph, at 29 °C the rate of reaction is 0.08 s^{-1}. The time taken is the reciprocal of the rate. That is:

$$\text{time taken} = \frac{1}{0.08}$$

$$= \textbf{12.5 s}$$

(b) The rate is the reciprocal of time. So, if the reaction took 25 s for the colour change to take place, the rate is expressed by:

$$\text{rate} = \frac{1}{25}$$

$$= \textbf{0.04 s}^{-1}$$

From the graph, the reaction has a rate of 0.04 s^{-1} when the temperature is **20 °C**.

PROBLEMS 7.11 – 7.15

Problems 7.11 – 7.15 are of the type illustrated in Worked Examples 7.3 and 7.4.

7.11 The graph below shows how the rate of a clock reaction varies with the concentration at which it is carried out. The rate is expressed as the reciprocal of the time taken for a colour change to appear.

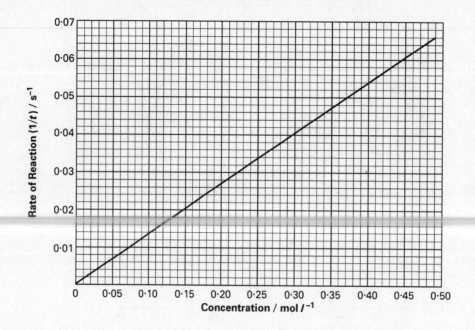

(a) At what concentration does the colour change take 20 s to occur?

(b) After what time will the colour change take place if the reaction is carried out at a concentration of 0.15 mol l^{-1}?

7.12 The graph below shows how the rate of a clock reaction varies with the temperature at which it is carried out. The rate is expressed as the reciprocal of the time taken for cloudiness to appear.

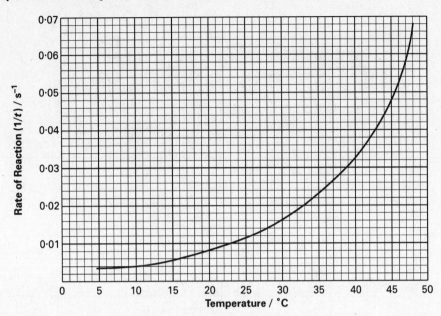

(a)   At what time will the cloudiness appear at a temperature of 43 °C?

(b)   At what temperature will the cloudiness appear after 50 s?

(c)   Obtain from the graph the values for the rate of reaction at 10 °C, 20 °C, 30 °C and 40 °C. What relationship between the temperatures and the rates can be observed?

7.13 The graph below shows how the rate of a clock reaction varies with the concentration at which it is carried out. The rate is expressed as the reciprocal of the time taken for a colour change to appear.

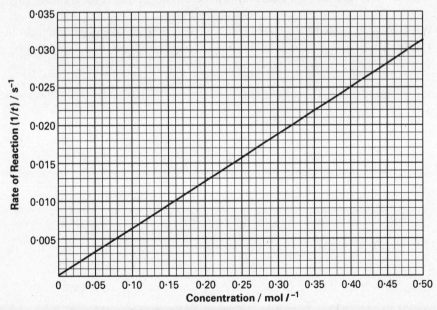

(a)   What concentration of reactant will cause the colour change in this reaction to take place after 50 s?

(b)   At what time will the colour change take place if the reagent concentration is 0·40 mol l^{-1}?

7.14 The graph below shows how the rate of a clock reaction varies with the temperature at which it is carried out. The rate is expressed as the reciprocal of the time taken for a colour change to appear.

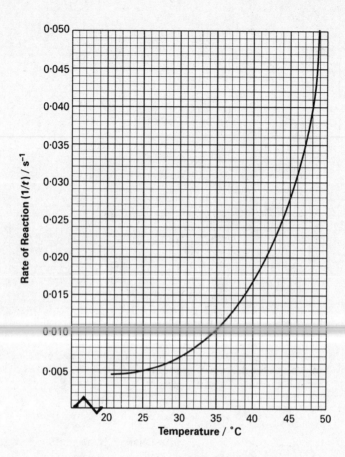

(a) At what temperature will the colour change take place 200 s after the reagents are mixed?

(b) At what time after the reagents are mixed will the colour change take place when the temperature of the solution is 48 °C?

7.15 The graph below shows how the rate of a clock reaction varies with the concentration at which it is carried out. The rate is expressed as the reciprocal of the time taken for a colour change to appear.

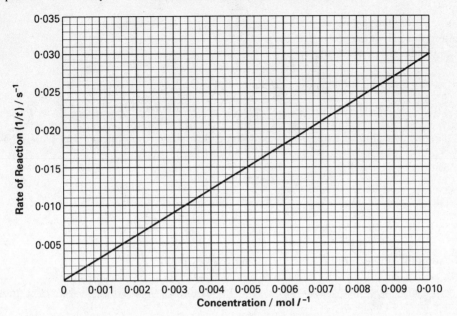

(a) How long will the colour change take to appear if the reagent concentration is 0·0054 mol l^{-1}?

(b) At what concentration of reagent will the colour change take 40 s to appear?

8. pH CALCULATIONS

In earlier work, the pH scale was introduced as a numerical scale from 0 to 14 which was a convenient way of describing the acidity or alkalinity of a solution.

* acid solutions had pH values below 7
* alkaline solutions had pH values above 7
* neutral solutions had a pH value of exactly 7

We now need to use a more precise, mathematical, definition of pH. It is

$$pH = -\log[H^+] \quad \text{(where $[H^+]$ means "the concentration of H^+ in mol l^{-1}")}$$

The point of this apparently complicated expression will become clear when some calculations using it have been carried out.

WORKED EXAMPLE 8.1

What is the pH of a solution in which the H^+ concentration is 0.001 mol l^{-1}?

For those familiar with using the special functions on scientific calculators, the calculation is simple; those less familiar may find the following approach helpful.

Firstly, write down the definition of pH. (This is partly to remind you what it is you are calculating and partly so that, in an examination, you may get *some* marks even if you get the final answer wrong.)

$$pH = -\log[H^+]$$

Then enter the value for the H^+ concentration (0.001) into your calculator.

The process of converting this concentration to pH is a two step process:

1. Firstly we take the log of this value. Press the "log" button of your calculator. This will produce the number -3 on the display.

2. Now take the negative of this value; this is the same as changing the sign (if any) in front of the number. This is usually done with the key marked:

    $\boxed{+/_-}$

    So we now get the value 3.

Thus the pH of the solution is 3.

Now that we have the answer to the problem, we can see what the point of pH numbers is; by using the "log" function, we have changed a fairly unwieldy number into a simple one. The use of the negative was to make sure that we (usually) end up with a positive pH number. It is much easier to describe a solution as "being pH 3" than saying that it has "a hydrogen ion concentration of 0.001 mol l^{-1}"!

WORKED EXAMPLE 8.2

What is the pH of a solution in which the H⁺ concentration is $2 \cdot 5 \times 10^{-3}$ mol l^{-1}?

This problem is no different from the previous one except that [H⁺] is given in "standard form" or "scientific notation". We proceed as before.

$$pH = -\log[H^+]$$

The value for [H⁺], that is $2 \cdot 5 \times 10^{-3}$, is entered in the calculator. Then:

1.   The log button is pressed. The display now reads $-2 \cdot 60206$.
2.   The sign is changed, giving $2 \cdot 60$ (after rounding)

So the pH of the solution is $2 \cdot 60$, rounded to 3 significant figures.

WORKED EXAMPLE 8.3

What is the pH of a $0 \cdot 05$ mol l^{-1} solution of sulphuric acid, H_2SO_4?

On the surface, this problem looks no different from the previous ones. However, we are not told the concentration of H⁺ directly; instead we are told the concentration of the acid, in this case, sulphuric. Now sulphuric acid, H_2SO_4, produces **2 mol** of H⁺ for every **1 mol** of acid, since the formula for the acid contains **2** H atoms able to form ions in solution. So the concentration of H⁺ ions is **twice** the concentration of the acid. That is:

$$[H^+] = 2 \times 0 \cdot 05 = 0 \cdot 1 \text{ mol } l^{-1}$$

We then proceed as before.

$$pH = -\log[H^+]$$

The value $0 \cdot 1$ is entered in the calculator. Then:

1.   The log of this value is taken. The value -1 appears on the display.
2.   The sign is changed, giving us the value 1.

Thus, the pH of the solution is 1.

WORKED EXAMPLE 8.4

What is the pH of a solution of 1 mol l^{-1} sulphuric acid, H_2SO_4?

As in the previous worked example, we change the concentration of the acid into the concentration of H⁺.

$$[H^+] = 2 \times 1 = 2 \text{ mol } l^{-1}$$

$$pH = -\log[H^+]$$

The value of [H⁺] = 2 is entered in the calculator. Then:

1.   The log of this value is taken. The display now reads $0 \cdot 30103$.
2.   The sign is changed, giving us $-0 \cdot 301$ (after rounding).

So the pH is $-0 \cdot 301$, rounded to 3 significant figures.

This is the first example, so far, of a **negative** pH value. Although the pH values of most solutions are positive, negative values will be obtained when [H⁺] is above 1 mol l^{-1}.

PROBLEMS 8.1 to 8.10

Problems 8.1 to 8.10 are of the type shown in Worked Examples 8.1 to 8.4, in which pH is calculated from a given concentration, either of H⁺ ions or of a specified acid.

8. 1 Calculate the pH of a solution in which the concentration of H^+ ions is 0.1 mol l^{-1}.

8. 2 Calculate the pH of a solution in which the concentration of hydrogen ions is 0.05 mol l^{-1}.

8. 3 A solution has a hydrogen ion concentration of 0.4 mol l^{-1}. Calculate the pH of the solution.

8. 4 The concentration of H^+ ions in a solution is 6.2×10^{-8} mol l^{-1}. Calculate the pH of the solution.

8. 5 A weak acid solution has a hydrogen ion concentration of 3.8×10^{-5} mol l^{-1}. Calculate the pH of the solution

8. 6 Calculate the pH of a 0.02 mol l^{-1} solution of hydrochloric acid, HCl.

8. 7 Calculate the pH of a 0.4 mol l^{-1} solution of sulphuric acid, H_2SO_4.

8. 8 Calculate the pH of a 0.01 mol l^{-1} solution of nitric acid, HNO_3.

8. 9 Calculate the pH of a 0.02 mol l^{-1} solution of sulphuric acid, H_2SO_4.

8.10 Calculate the pH of a 1.2 mol l^{-1} solution of sulphuric acid, H_2SO_4.

WORKED EXAMPLE 8.5

The pH of a solution is 4·5. What is the concentration of H⁺?

In this problem, we are given the pH and asked the concentration; the opposite of the previous examples. The method is essentially the same as before except that we carry out the opposite of the 2 stages of calculation. Whereas before we firstly took the log and then changed the sign, now we start by changing the sign and then taking the opposite of log; the inverse log. (On most calculators, inverse log is designated as "10ˣ" and is obtained by entering the number and then pressing the "INV" button followed by the "log" button.)

$$pH = -\log[H^+]$$

The pH value of 4·5 is entered in the calculator. Then:

1. Change the sign. So the display now reads –4·5
2. Press the button(s) which give inverse log. The display now reads 3.16×10^{-5} (rounded).

Thus, the concentration of hydrogen ions is 3.16×10^{-5} mol l^{-1}, rounded to 3 significant figures.

WORKED EXAMPLE 8.6

A solution of sulphuric acid, H_2SO_4, has a pH of 3·4. Calculate:

(a) **the concentration of H^+ ions and**

(b) **the concentration of the sulphuric acid.**

(a) The first part of this is no different from that of Worked Example 8.5.

$$pH = -\log[H^+]$$

The pH of 3·4 is entered in a calculator. Then:

       1.   The sign is changed. The display reads −3·4.
       2.   The inverse log of this value is taken. The display reads $3·98 \times 10^{-4}$ (rounded).

So the concentration of H^+ ions is $3·98 \times 10^{-4}$ mol l^{-1}.

(b) In Worked Example 8.3, it was noted that in a solution of sulphuric acid, H_2SO_4, the concentration of H^+ ions is **twice** that of the acid. So, in this example we can say that:

If the concentration of H^+ ions is $3·98 \times 10^{-4}$ mol l^{-1}, the concentration of the acid is:

$$\frac{3·98 \times 10^{-4}}{2} \ \text{mol}\ l^{-1}$$

$$= \ 1·99 \times 10^{-4} \ \text{mol}\ l^{-1}, \text{rounded to 3 significant figures.}$$

PROBLEMS 8.11 to 8.20

Problems 8.11 to 8.20 are of the type shown in Worked Examples 8.5 and 8.6, in which pH is given and the concentration of H^+ and, in some cases, that of a specified acid, has to be calculated.

8.11   Calculate the concentration of H^+ ions in a solution with a pH of 11·5.

8.12   What is the concentration of H^+ ions in a solution of an alkali which has a pH of 12·9?

8.13   A dilute solution of hydrochloric acid has a pH of −0·15. What is the concentration of the H^+ ions in the solution?

8.14   A solution of lactic acid has a pH of 4·8. Calculate the concentration of H^+ ions.

8.15   A solution of nitric acid has a pH of 3·5. Calculate the concentration of H^+ ions.

8.16   A dilute solution of sulphuric acid, H_2SO_4, has a pH of 2·8. Calculate *(a)* the concentration of H^+ ions and *(b)* the concentration of the acid.

8.17   A solution of nitric acid, HNO_3, has a pH of 1·5. Calculate *(a)* the concentration of H^+ ions and *(b)* the concentration of the acid.

8.18   A solution of sulphuric acid, H_2SO_4, has a pH of 3·2. Calculate *(a)* the concentration of H^+ ions and *(b)* the concentration of the acid.

8.19   A solution of hydrochloric acid, HCl, has a pH of 1·8. Calculate *(a)* the concentration of H^+ ions and *(b)* the concentration of the acid.

8.20   A solution of sulphuric acid, H_2SO_4, has a pH of −0·2. Calculate *(a)* the concentration of H^+ ions and *(b)* the concentration of the acid.

ADDITIONAL THEORY

A feature of all aqueous solutions, whether acid, alkaline or neutral, is that they contain H^+ and OH^- ions in equilibrium with each other. At 25 °C, the mathematical relationship below applies to all such solutions.

$$[H^+][OH^-] = 10^{-14} \ \text{mol}^2 \ l^{-2}$$

This relationship means that (at 25 °C), if we know the concentration of H^+, we can calculate the concentration of OH^-, and *vice versa*. This can be seen in the following Worked Examples.

WORKED EXAMPLE 8.7

A solution has a hydroxide ion concentration of 2×10^{-11} mol l^{-1}. What is *(a)* the hydrogen ion concentration and *(b)* the pH of the solution?

(a) We write the equation connecting the concentrations of H^+ and OH^-.

$$[H^+][OH^-] = 10^{-14}$$

We then rewrite the equation to leave $[H^+]$ on the left, insert the data and calculate $[H^+]$.

$$[H^+] = \frac{10^{-14}}{[OH^-]} = \frac{10^{-14}}{2 \times 10^{-11}} = 5 \times 10^{-4}$$

So $[H^+] = 5 \times 10^{-4}$ mol l^{-1}

(b) We obtain the pH from the calculated $[H^+]$ as in previous Worked Examples:

$$pH = -\log[H^+]$$

The value for $[H^+]$ of 5×10^{-4} is entered on the calculator. Then:

1. The log is taken. The display reads $-3 \cdot 30$ (rounded)
2. The sign is changed to give $3 \cdot 30$.

So the pH of the solution is $3 \cdot 30$, to 3 significant figures.

WORKED EXAMPLE 8.8

A solution has a pH of 5·3. Calculate *(a)* the [H⁺] and *(b)* the [OH⁻] of the solution.

(a) The conversion of the pH value to [H⁺] uses the method shown in Worked Example 8.5.

$$pH = -\log[H^+]$$

The number 5·3 is entered in the calculator. Then:

1. The sign is changed. The display now reads –5·3.
2. The inverse log is taken. The display now reads $5·01 \times 10^{-6}$ (rounded)

So the [H⁺] is $5·01 \times 10^{-6}$ mol l^{-1}.

(b) We write the equation connecting [H⁺] and [OH⁻].

$$[H^+][OH^-] = 10^{-14}$$

We then rewrite the equation to give [OH⁻] on the left, insert the data and calculate:

$$[OH^-] = \frac{10^{-14}}{[H^+]} = \frac{10^{-14}}{5·01 \times 10^{-6}} = 2·00 \times 10^{-9} \text{ (rounded)}$$

So the [OH⁻] is $2·00 \times 10^{-9}$ mol l^{-1}, rounded to 3 significant figures.

PROBLEMS 8.21 to 8.30

Problems 8.21 to 8.30 are of the type shown in Worked Examples 8.7 and 8.8, involving the use of the equation $[H^+][OH^-] = 10^{-14}$ in addition to pH calculations. Assume that solutions are at 25 °C (the temperature at which this equation applies) in these problems.

8.21 A solution of an alkali has a pH of 12. Calculate the concentration of *(a)* H⁺ ions and *(b)* OH⁻ ions.

8.22 A weak acid solution has an H⁺ ion concentration of 10^{-4} mol l^{-1}. Calculate *(a)* the pH and *(b)* the concentration of OH⁻ ions.

8.23 An acid solution has a OH⁻ ion concentration of 2×10^{-13} mol l^{-1}. Calculate *(a)* the concentration of H⁺ ions and *(b)* the pH.

8.24 A weakly alkaline solution has a pH of 8·4. Calculate *(a)* the concentration of H⁺ ions and *(b)* the concentration of OH⁻ ions.

8.25 The H⁺ ion concentration of a solution is $3·4 \times 10^{-3}$ mol l^{-1}. Calculate *(a)* the pH and *(b)* the concentration of OH⁻ ions.

8.26 The OH⁻ ion concentration of a solution is $6·3 \times 10^{-12}$ mol l^{-1}. Calculate *(a)* the concentration of H⁺ ions and *(b)* the pH.

8.27 The pH of a strong acid solution is –0·25. Calculate *(a)* the concentration of H⁺ ions and *(b)* the concentration of OH⁻ ions.

8.28 The H⁺ ion concentration of an acid solution is $4·4 \times 10^{-4}$ mol l^{-1}. Calculate *(a)* the pH and *(b)* the concentration of OH⁻ ions.

8.29 The OH⁻ ion concentration of a solution is 0·02 mol l^{-1}. Calculate *(a)* the concentration of H⁺ ions and *(b)* the pH.

8.30 The pH of a solution is 3·4. Calculate *(a)* the concentration of H⁺ ions and *(b)* the concentration of OH⁻ ions.

9.   MEASURING ΔH EXPERIMENTALLY

The enthalpy change, ΔH, for a chemical reaction is expressed as the amount of heat energy (in kJ) given out or taken in for every mole of a particular substance reacted or product formed.

We can measure the heat given out or taken in during certain reactions by using it to increase or decrease the temperature of a known mass of water. We can then use the equation below to calculate the amount of heat involved:

$$\Delta H = cm\Delta T$$

In this equation,

- ΔH is the heat given out or taken in during the reaction. This is measured in kilojoules (kJ).

- c is a constant, called the specific heat capacity, for the substance being heated or cooled. In all the examples we will consider, the substance will be water (or mainly water) and we will use the value $c = 4\cdot18$ kJ kg^{-1} K^{-1} (kilojoules for every kg of water heated by 1 degree Kelvin).

- m is the mass, in kg, of water being heated.

- ΔT is the temperature change. Although the unit for temperature is officially the Kelvin (K), the size of a Kelvin degree is the same as a Celsius (or Centigrade) degree (°C). This means that a given temperature change measured in Kelvin is the same as that measured in Celsius. In this chapter, temperatures and temperature changes will be measured in Celsius degrees, being the more commonly used unit of temperature.

The use of this equation can be seen in the following Worked Examples.

WORKED EXAMPLE 9.1

A substance is dissolved in 0·3 kg of water, causing a temperature rise of 5 °C. What quantity of heat has been given out?

In this problem,

$$m \quad = \quad 0\cdot3 \text{ kg}$$
$$c \quad = \quad 4\cdot18 \text{ kJ kg}^{-1} \text{ K}^{-1}$$
$$\Delta T \quad = \quad 5 \text{ °C}$$

We fit these figures into the equation shown below:

$$\Delta H \quad = \quad cm\Delta T$$
$$= \quad 4\cdot18 \times 0\cdot3 \times 5$$
$$= \quad \textbf{6·27 kJ}$$

This calculated value is the quantity of heat given out in the dissolving process described.

WORKED EXAMPLE 9.2

0·02 mol of a substance is burned in a spirit burner. The heat given out is used to raise the temperature of 0·4 kg of water by 10 °C. Calculate the Enthalpy of Combustion of the alcohol.

The Enthalpy of Combustion of a compound is the quantity of heat given out when **1 mol** of the compound is burned completely.

Firstly, we calculate the quantity of heat produced:

$$
\begin{aligned}
\Delta H \quad &= \quad cm\Delta T \\
&= \quad 4\!\cdot\!18 \times 0\!\cdot\!4 \times 10 \\
&= \quad 16\!\cdot\!72 \text{ kJ}
\end{aligned}
$$

This is the amount of heat given out when **0·02 mol** of the compound was burned. We now calculate the amount of heat which would be given out if **1 mol** had been burned.

$$0\!\cdot\!02 \text{ mol burns giving out } 16\!\cdot\!72 \text{ kJ of heat}$$

$$1 \text{ mol burns giving out } \frac{16\!\cdot\!72}{0\!\cdot\!02} \text{ kJ of heat}$$

$$= \quad \textbf{836 kJ}$$

So the Enthalpy of Combustion of the substance is −836 kJ mol⁻¹.

Note that the negative sign is included to show that this is heat given out; that is, it is an exothermic reaction. Be aware, however, that some text books and data books do not include the negative sign before combustion enthalpies. (Since combustions are **always** exothermic, it is argued that the sign is therefore not necessary, except when carrying out the kind of calculations shown in Chapter 10.) In this book, however, the signs showing the direction of enthalpy changes will **always** be shown.

WORKED EXAMPLE 9.3

0·3 mol of a salt is dissolved in 0·25 kg of water, causing a rise in the temperature of the solution from 17 °C to 23 °C. Calculate the Enthalpy of Solution of the salt.

The Enthalpy of Solution is the quantity of heat given out or taken in when 1 mol of a particular substance is dissolved completely in water.

Firstly, we calculate the quantity of heat produced, remembering that ΔT is the change in temperature which, in this example, is 6 °C.

$$
\begin{aligned}
\Delta H \quad &= \quad cm\Delta T \\
&= \quad 4\!\cdot\!18 \times 0\!\cdot\!25 \times 6 \\
&= \quad 6\!\cdot\!27 \text{ kJ}
\end{aligned}
$$

This is the amount of heat given out when 0·3 mol of the salt dissolves.

We now calculate the amount of heat which would be given out if **1 mol** were dissolved.

$$0.3 \text{ mol dissolves, giving out} \quad 6.27 \quad \text{kJ of heat}$$

$$1 \quad \text{mol dissolves, giving out} \quad \frac{6.27}{0.3} \quad \text{kJ of heat}$$

$$= \quad \textbf{20.9 kJ}$$

So the Enthalpy of Solution of the salt is −20.9 kJ mol⁻¹.

The more observant student will have noticed that what is being heated up in this Worked Example is not pure water, but a salt solution. Can the value for the specific heat capacity of **water** ($c = 4.18$ kJ kg⁻¹ K⁻¹) therefore be used in the calculation? Strictly speaking, the answer is no, but since the solution formed is very dilute, we can assume, within the limits of the accuracy of this experiment, that we are dealing with pure water.

WORKED EXAMPLE 9.4

0.16 g of methanol, CH₃OH, is burned in a spirit burner. The heat from this combustion causes the temperature of 0.1 kg of water to be raised from 20 °C to 27 °C. Use this information to calculate the Enthalpy of Combustion of methanol.

Fitting the data into the equation, we have:

$$
\begin{aligned}
\Delta H &= cm\Delta T \\
&= 4.18 \times 0.1 \times 7 \\
&= 2.926 \text{ kJ}
\end{aligned}
$$

The calculated value of 2.926 kJ is the quantity of heat which is given out when 0.16 g of methanol is burned.

We now calculate the heat which would have been given out if **1 mol** of methanol had been burned.

The formula of methanol is CH₃OH. So 1 mol of methanol = 32 g

$$0.16 \text{ g of methanol burns giving out} \quad 2.926 \quad \text{kJ of heat}$$

$$1 \quad \text{g of methanol burns giving out} \quad \frac{2.926}{0.16} \quad \text{kJ of heat}$$

$$32 \quad \text{g of methanol burns giving out} \quad \frac{2.926 \times 32}{0.16} \quad \text{kJ of heat}$$

$$= \quad \textbf{585.2 kJ}$$

Thus, the calculated Enthalpy of Combustion of methanol is −585.2 kJ mol⁻¹.

WORKED EXAMPLE 9.5

4 g of ammonium nitrate, NH_4NO_3, is dissolved completely in 100 cm^3 of water in an insulated container. The temperature of the water falls from 19 °C to 16 °C. Calculate the Enthalpy of Solution of ammonium nitrate.

Note that in this problem, the **volume** of water is given rather than the **mass**. Since it is known that 1 litre (1000 cm^3) of water weighs 1 kg (1000 g), the conversion of 100 cm^3 to 0·1 kg is straightforward.

The data are now put into the equation:

$$\begin{aligned} \Delta H &= cm\Delta T \\ &= 4{\cdot}18 \times 0{\cdot}1 \times 3 \\ &= 1{\cdot}254 \text{ kJ} \end{aligned}$$

The calculated value of 1·254 kJ is the quantity of heat taken in by 4 g of ammonium nitrate from the water. We now need to obtain the quantity of heat which would be taken in by **1 mol** of ammonium nitrate.

The formula of ammonium nitrate is NH_4NO_3. So 1 mol of NH_4NO_3 = 80 g.

4 g of ammonium nitrate dissolves, taking in	1·254	kJ of heat
1 g of ammonium nitrate dissolves, taking in	$\dfrac{1{\cdot}254}{4{\cdot}0}$	kJ of heat
80 g of ammonium nitrate dissolves, taking in	$\dfrac{1{\cdot}254 \times 80}{4{\cdot}0}$	kJ of heat
	= **25·08 kJ**	

So the calculated Enthalpy of Solution of ammonium nitrate is +25·1 kJ mol^{-1}.

WORKED EXAMPLE 9.6

100 cm^3 of 1 mol l^{-1} hydrochloric acid solution and 100 cm^3 of 1 mol l^{-1} sodium hydroxide solution (both at 20 °C) are mixed in an insulated container. The temperature of the solution rises to 27 °C. Calculate the Enthalpy of Neutralisation from this information.

When mixed, the total volume of solution will be 200 cm^3 which has a mass of 0·2 kg.

This, and the other data can be put into the equation:

$$\begin{aligned} \Delta H &= cm\Delta T \\ &= 4{\cdot}18 \times 0{\cdot}2 \times 7 \\ &= 5{\cdot}852 \text{ kJ} \end{aligned}$$

The Enthalpy of Neutralisation is defined as the quantity of heat given out when **1 mol** of water is formed in the neutralisation of a strong acid and a strong alkali. What we have calculated is the amount of heat given out when 0·1 mol of HCl neutralises 0·1 mol of NaOH. This results in the formation of 0·1 mol of water as can be seen from the balanced chemical equation below:

	NaOH	+	HCl	⟶	NaCl	+	H_2O
	1 mol	+	1 mol		1 mol	+	1 mol
So	0·1 mol	+	0·1 mol		0·1 mol	+	0·1 mol

0·1 mol of water is formed, giving out   5·852   kJ of heat

1   mol of water is formed, giving out $\dfrac{5\cdot852}{0\cdot1}$ kJ of heat

=   **58·52 kJ**

That is, the calculated Enthalpy of Neutralisation is −58·52 kJ mol⁻¹.

PROBLEMS 9.1. to 9.25

■ **Problems 9.1 to 9.5 involve simple calculations of the type shown in Worked Example 9.1.**

■ **Problems 9.6 to 9.10 involve calculations of the Enthalpies of Solution and Combustion of the type shown in Worked Examples 9.2 and 9.3.**

■ **Problems 9.11 to 9.20 involve calculations of the Enthalpies of Solution and Combustion of the type shown in Worked Examples 9.4 and 9.5.**

■ **Problems 9.21 to 9.25 involve calculations of the Enthalpy of Neutralisation of the type shown in Worked Example 9.6.**

9. 1   A substance is dissolved in 0·2 kg of water, causing a temperature rise of 4 °C. What quantity of heat has been given out?

9. 2   A certain mass of alcohol is burned in a spirit burner which is used to heat up 0·1 kg of water in a metal can. The temperature of the water rises by 8 °C. What quantity of heat has been given out?

9. 3   A 3 °C fall in temperature is recorded when a substance is dissolved in 0·25 kg of water. What quantity of heat has been absorbed by the water?

9. 4   When a quantity of a substance is dissolved in 0·2 kg of water, the temperature rises from 19·5 °C to 21 °C. What quantity of heat has been given out?

9. 5   A Bunsen burner is used to heat 0·5 kg of water from 20·5 °C to 39·5 °C. How much heat has been produced in the burning of the gas?

9. 6   0·01 mol of a substance is dissolved in 0·2 kg of water, causing the temperature to drop from 19 °C to 17 °C. Calculate the Enthalpy of Solution of the substance.

9. 7   0·02 mol of a hydrocarbon is burned completely in air and the heat produced is used to heat 0·1 kg of water from 20·5 °C to 29·5 °C. Calculate the Enthalpy of Combustion of the fuel.

9. 8   0·025 mol of a salt is dissolved in 0·4 kg of water at 20 °C. The temperature of the solution rises to 25 °C. Calculate the Enthalpy of Solution of the salt.

9. 9 A can containing 0·1 kg of water at 21 °C is heated to 29 °C when a burner containing an alcohol is lit underneath it. If 0·02 mol of the alcohol is burned in the process, calculate its Enthalpy of Combustion.

9.10 0·05 mol of a compound is dissolved in 0·5 kg of water, causing its temperature to fall from 21 °C to 19·5 °C. Calculate the Enthalpy of Solution of the compound.

9.11 0·32 g of methanol, CH_3OH, is burned in a spirit burner which is used to heat up 0·2 kg of water from 19·5 °C to 27·5 °C. Calculate the Enthalpy of Combustion of methanol.

9.12 5·3 g of sodium carbonate, Na_2CO_3, is dissolved in 0·1 kg of water, causing the temperature to rise from 20·5 °C to 23·5 °C. Calculate the Enthalpy of Solution of the compound.

9.13 The burning of 0·2 g of methane, CH_4, is used to raise the temperature of 0·25 kg of water from 18·5 °C to 28·5 °C. Calculate the Enthalpy of Combustion of methane.

9.14 8 g of ammonium nitrate, NH_4NO_3, is dissolved in 0·2 kg of water, causing the temperature to drop from 20 °C to 17 °C. Calculate the Enthalpy of Solution of ammonium nitrate.

9.15 A burner containing ethanol, C_2H_5OH, is used to heat up 0·4 kg of water from 21 °C to 37 °C. In the process, 0·92 g of ethanol is burned. Calculate the Enthalpy of Combustion of ethanol.

9.16 4 g of sodium hydroxide, $NaOH$, is dissolved in 0·25 kg of water, causing the temperature to rise from 19 °C to 23 °C. Calculate the Enthalpy of Solution of sodium hydroxide.

9.17 0·22 g of propane, C_3H_8, is burned to heat 0·25 kg of water from 21 °C to 31 °C. Calculate the Enthalpy of Combustion of propane.

9.18 14·9 g of potassium chloride, KCl, is dissolved in 0·2 kg of water. The temperature falls from 19·5 °C to 15·5 °C. Calculate the Enthalpy of Solution of the Salt.

9.19 A gas burner containing butane, C_4H_{10}, is used to heat 0·15 kg of water from 22·5 °C to 31 °C. 0·116 g of butane is burned in the process. Calculate the Enthalpy of Combustion of butane.

9.20 2·525 g of potassium nitrate, KNO_3, is dissolved in 0·1 kg of water, causing the temperature to fall from 20·5 °C to 18·5 °C. Calculate the Enthalpy of Solution of potassium nitrate.

9.21 100 cm^3 of 0·5 mol l^{-1} nitric acid, HNO_3, and 100 cm^3 of 0·5 mol l^{-1} potassium hydroxide solution, KOH (both solutions at the same temperature) are mixed in an insulated container. A temperature rise of 3·5 °C is noted. Calculate the Enthalpy of Neutralisation.

9.22 50 cm^3 of 1 mol l^{-1} hydrochloric acid, HCl, and 50 cm^3 of 1 mol l^{-1} potassium hydroxide solution, KOH, both at 20 °C, are mixed. The temperature of the resulting solution rises to 26·9 °C. Calculate the Enthalpy of Neutralisation.

9.23 40 cm^3 of 1 mol l^{-1} of nitric acid, HNO_3, and 40 cm^3 of 1 mol l^{-1} sodium hydroxide, $NaOH$, are allowed to reach room temperature of 19 °C. When the solutions are mixed, the temperature rises to 25·8 °C. Calculate the Enthalpy of Neutralisation.

9.24 80 cm^3 of 0·5 mol l^{-1} of potassium hydroxide solution, KOH, and 80 cm^3 of 0·5 mol l^{-1} hydrochloric acid, HCl, both at 18·5 °C, are mixed. The temperature of the resulting solution rises to 21·9 °C. Calculate the Enthalpy of Neutralisation.

9.25 25 cm^3 of 1 mol l^{-1} sulphuric acid, H_2SO_4, is neutralised by 50 cm^3 of 1 mol l^{-1} sodium hydroxide solution, $NaOH$. A temperature rise of 9·1 °C is noted. Calculate the Enthalpy of Neutralisation.

WORKED EXAMPLES 9.7 – 9.9

These next Worked Examples, and the problems which follow, are slightly more complex and need more arithmetical manipulation than those previously considered.

WORKED EXAMPLE 9.7

The Enthalpy of Solution of sodium carbonate, Na_2CO_3, is $-24·7$ kJ mol^{-1}. What mass of sodium carbonate dissolved in 150 cm^3 of water would cause a temperature rise of 0·5 °C?

We firstly calculate the amount of heat given out:

$$\Delta H = cm\Delta T$$
$$= 4·18 \times 0·15 \times 0·5$$
$$= 0·3135 \text{ kJ}$$

Next, we note that:

The Enthalpy of Solution of Na_2CO_3 is $-24·7$ kJ mol^{-1} and 1 mol of Na_2CO_3 = 106 g.

So

24·7	kJ is the heat given out when	106	g of Na_2CO_3 dissolves
1	kJ is the heat given out when	$\dfrac{106}{24·7}$	g of Na_2CO_3 dissolves
0·3135	kJ is the heat given out when	$\dfrac{106 \times 0·3135}{24·7}$	g of Na_2CO_3 dissolves

$$= \mathbf{1·345 \text{ g}} \text{ (after rounding)}$$

WORKED EXAMPLE 9.8

The Enthalpy of Combustion of methanol is -715 kJ mol^{-1}. A burner containing methanol, CH_3OH, is used to heat up 400 cm^3 of water. What temperature rise would be produced in the water if 0·64 g of methanol were completely burned?

In this problem, we cannot use the equation $\Delta H = cm\Delta T$ immediately, because we are asked for the temperature rise, ΔT, but we do not yet know ΔH — the heat given out in this particular experiment. We firstly have to calculate ΔH from the Enthalpy of Combustion value given.

The Enthalpy of Combustion of $CH_3OH = -715$ kJ mol^{-1} and 1 mol of CH_3OH = 32 g

So we can calculate the amount of heat given out (ΔH) when 0·64 g burns as follows:

32	g of CH_3OH burns, giving out	715	kJ of heat
1	g of CH_3OH burns giving out	$\dfrac{715}{32}$	kJ of heat
0·64	g of CH_3OH burns giving out	$\dfrac{715 \times 0·64}{32}$	kJ of heat

$$= 14·28 \text{ kJ}$$

We can now put this value for ΔH, and the other known values, into the equation ΔH = cmΔT, after rearranging it to put ΔT on the left hand side.

$$\Delta H = cm\Delta T$$

So:
$$\Delta T = \frac{\Delta H}{cm}$$

$$= \frac{14 \cdot 28}{4 \cdot 18 \times 0 \cdot 4}$$

$$= \mathbf{8 \cdot 541} \text{ °C (after rounding)}$$

WORKED EXAMPLE 9.9

50 cm³ of 0·2 mol l^{-1} sodium hydroxide solution, NaOH, is neutralised by 50 cm³ of 0·2 mol l^{-1} hydrochloric acid, HCl. Calculate the resulting temperature rise. (Take the Enthalpy of Neutralisation to be –57·3 kJ mol^{-1}.)

We firstly calculate how many moles of water have been formed in the neutralisation.

No. of moles of NaOH = 0·05 × 0·2 = 0·01 mol

No. of moles of HCl = 0·05 × 0·2 = 0·01 mol

	HCl	+	NaOH	⟶	NaCl	+	H₂O
	1 mol	+	1 mol		1 mol	+	1 mol
So:	0·01 mol	+	0·01 mol		0·01 mol	+	0·01 mol

So 0·01 mol of water has been formed in this neutralisation. We can then use the value given for the Enthalpy of Neutralisation to calculate how much heat (ΔH) would have been given out in this particular case.

1 mol of water is formed, giving out 57·3 kJ of heat

0·01 mol of water is formed, giving out 0·01 × 57·3 kJ of heat

$$= 0 \cdot 573 \text{ kJ}$$

We can now put this value for ΔH, and the other known values, into the equation ΔH = cmΔT, after rearranging it to put ΔT on the left hand side.

$$\Delta H = cm\Delta T$$

So
$$\Delta T = \frac{\Delta H}{cm}$$

$$= \frac{0 \cdot 573}{4 \cdot 18 \times 0 \cdot 1}$$

$$= \mathbf{1 \cdot 371} \text{ °C (after rounding)}$$

PROBLEMS 9.26 to 9.40

- ■ **Problems 9.26 to 9.35 are of the type shown in Worked Examples 9.7 and 9.8, involving Enthalpies of Solution and Combustion.**
- ■ **Problems 9.36 to 9.40 are of the type shown in Worked 9.9, involving the Enthalpy of Neutralisation.**

9.26   The Enthalpy of Solution of sodium hydroxide, NaOH, is $-42 \cdot 6$ kJ mol^{-1}. What mass of sodium hydroxide would produce a temperature rise of 5 °C when dissolved completely in 200 cm^3 of water?

9.27   The Enthalpy of Combustion of ethanol, C_2H_5OH, is -1371 kJ mol^{-1}. If a spirit burner containing ethanol was used to heat a can of water, what mass of ethanol would raise the temperature of 300 cm^3 of water by 10 °C?

9.28   The Enthalpy of Solution of sodium carbonate, Na_2CO_3, is $-24 \cdot 7$ kJ mol^{-1}. Calculate the temperature change which would take place if $1 \cdot 325$ g of sodium carbonate were dissolved completely in 250 cm^3 of water.

9.29   The Enthalpy of Combustion of propanol is -2010 kJ mol^{-1}. A burner containing propanol, C_3H_7OH, is used to heat up 200 cm^3 of water. What mass of propanol would require to be burned to produce a temperature rise of $13 \cdot 5$ °C?

9.30   The Enthalpy of Solution of potassium hydroxide, KOH, is $-55 \cdot 2$ kJ mol^{-1}. What temperature change would take place if $2 \cdot 8$ g of potassium hydroxide were dissolved completely in 100 cm^3 of water?

9.31   A Bunsen burner uses methane, CH_4, which has an Enthalpy of Combustion of -882 kJ mol^{-1}. If $0 \cdot 4$ g of methane were completely burned to heat a can containing 500 cm^3 of water, what would be the maximum temperature rise which would be produced?

9.32   The Enthalpy of Solution of ammonium chloride, NH_4Cl, is $+15 \cdot 0$ kJ mol^{-1}. What mass of ammonium chloride would require to be dissolved in 200 cm^3 of water to lower the temperature by 2 °C?

9.33   The Enthalpy of Combustion of propane is -2202 kJ mol^{-1}. What would be the minimum mass of propane, C_3H_8, which would need to be completely burned in a propane burner to bring 5 kg of water to the boil from an initial temperature of 20 °C?

9.34   The Enthalpy of Solution of barium hydroxide, $Ba(OH)_2$, is $-51 \cdot 8$ kJ mol^{-1}. What mass of barium hydroxide dissolved in 200 cm^3 of water would cause a temperature rise of 4 °C?

9.35   A camping stove runs on butane, C_4H_{10}. If the Enthalpy of Combustion of butane is -2877 kJ mol^{-1}, what mass of butane would require to be burned to bring 2 kg of water to the boil from an initial temperature of 20 °C?

Note: In the following problems, take the Enthalpy of Neutralisation of a strong acid with a strong alkali to be $-57 \cdot 3$ kJ mol^{-1}.

9.36   60 cm^3 of $0 \cdot 5$ mol l^{-1} potassium hydroxide solution, KOH, is neutralised by 60 cm^3 of $0 \cdot 5$ mol l^{-1} hydrochloric acid, HCl. Calculate the temperature rise which would take place. (Assume both solutions were at the same temperature before mixing.)

9.37   30 cm^3 of 1 mol l^{-1} sodium hydroxide solution, NaOH, is neutralised by 30 cm^3 of 1 mol l^{-1} nitric acid, HNO_3. Calculate the resulting temperature rise. (Assume both solutions were at the same temperature before mixing.)

9.38   40 cm^3 of $0 \cdot 5$ mol l^{-1} potassium hydroxide solution, KOH, is neutralised by 40 cm^3 of $0 \cdot 5$ mol l^{-1} hydrochloric acid, HCl. Calculate the resulting temperature rise. (Assume both solutions were at the same temperature before mixing.)

9.39   80 cm^3 of $0 \cdot 5$ mol l^{-1} potassium hydroxide solution, KOH, is mixed with 80 cm^3 of $0 \cdot 5$ mol l^{-1} nitric acid, HNO_3. Calculate the resulting temperature rise. (Assume both solutions were at the same temperature before mixing.)

9.40   40 cm^3 of 1 mol l^{-1} sodium hydroxide solution, NaOH, is mixed with 20 cm^3 of 1 mol l^{-1} sulphuric acid, H_2SO_4. Calculate the temperature rise which would take place. (Assume both solutions were at the same temperature before mixing.)

10. HESS'S LAW USING EQUATIONS

Hess's Law of thermochemistry states (in simplified form) that the enthalpy change (ΔH) for a reaction depends only on the enthalpies of the reactants and the products and not on how the reaction is carried out or on how many steps are involved in the process.

An implication of this law is that if we can rearrange and combine chemical equations in such a way that we obtain a different equation, we can obtain the ΔH for the new reaction from the ΔH values of the original reactions. This idea seems complicated, but the following Worked Examples will clarify it.

WORKED EXAMPLE 10.1

Calculate the ΔH for the reaction below.

$$C \text{ (s)} \quad + \quad 2H_2 \text{ (g)} \quad \longrightarrow \quad CH_4 \text{ (g)}$$

Use the following data:

① $C \text{ (s)} \quad + \quad O_2 \text{ (g)} \quad \longrightarrow \quad CO_2 \text{ (g)}$ $\Delta H = -394 \text{ kJ mol}^{-1}$

② $H_2 \text{ (g)} \quad + \quad \frac{1}{2}O_2 \text{ (g)} \quad \longrightarrow \quad H_2O \text{ (}l\text{)}$ $\Delta H = -286 \text{ kJ mol}^{-1}$

③ $CH_4 \text{ (g)} \quad + \quad 2O_2 \text{ (g)} \quad \longrightarrow \quad CO_2 \text{ (g)} + 2H_2O \text{ (}l\text{)}$ $\Delta H = -882 \text{ kJ mol}^{-1}$

The basic technique is to rearrange the equations which we are told to use and to put them into a form which, when added together, will give us the required equation.

The equation we are trying to get to is the one below:

$$C \text{ (s)} \quad + \quad 2H_2\text{(g)} \quad \longrightarrow \quad CH_4 \text{ (g)}$$

The first substance on the left hand side (LHS) of this equation is C (s) so our first step is to find an equation in the ones we are told to use which contains C (s). The equation labelled ① has C (s) on the LHS, so we write it just as it is with its ΔH value alongside.

① $C \text{ (s)} \quad + \quad O_2 \text{ (g)} \quad \longrightarrow \quad CO_2 \text{ (g)}$ $\Delta H = -394 \text{ kJ mol}^{-1}$

The next substance that we want to help give us the required equation is $2H_2$ (g) on the LHS. Equation ② has H_2 (g) on the LHS, so this equation and its ΔH value are doubled. The equation is now represented as $2 \times$ ②.

$2 \times$ ② $2H_2 \text{ (g)} \quad + \quad O_2 \text{ (g)} \quad \longrightarrow \quad 2H_2O \text{ (}l\text{)}$ $\Delta H = -572 \text{ kJ mol}^{-1}$

The last substance we require is CH_4 (g) on the right hand side (RHS). CH_4 (g) is present in equation ③, but on the LHS, so we reverse this equation and change the sign of its ΔH value and write it as below as "– ③"

– ③ $CO_2 \text{ (g)} + 2H_2O \text{ (}l\text{)} \quad \longrightarrow \quad CH_4 \text{ (g)} + 2O_2 \text{ (g)}$ $\Delta H = +882 \text{ kJ mol}^{-1}$

Collecting these three equations together, we can then cancel out species common to both sides* and add them, and their ΔH values, together as shown below.

① $C \text{ (s)} \quad + \quad O_2 \text{ (g)} \quad \longrightarrow \quad CO_2 \text{ (g)}$ $\Delta H = -394 \text{ kJ mol}^{-1}$

$2 \times$ ② $2H_2 \text{ (g)} \quad + \quad O_2 \text{ (g)} \quad \longrightarrow \quad 2H_2O \text{ (}l\text{)}$ $\Delta H = -572 \text{ kJ mol}^{-1}$

– ③ $CO_2 \text{ (g)} \quad + \quad 2H_2O \text{ (}l\text{)} \quad \longrightarrow \quad CH_4 \text{ (g)} + 2O_2 \text{ (g)}$ $\Delta H = +882 \text{ kJ mol}^{-1}$

     $C \text{ (s)} \quad + \quad 2H_2 \text{ (g)} \quad \longrightarrow \quad CH_4 \text{ (g)}$ $\Delta H = \;\; -84 \text{ kJ mol}^{-1}$

---

* The cancelling took place as follows:

- Two O_2 (g), one from the LHS of the first equation and one from the LHS of the second equation, cancel with the $2O_2$ (g) on the RHS of the third equation.

- $2H_2O$ (l) appears on the RHS of the second equation and on the LHS of the third. They are cancelled.

- CO_2 (g) appears on the RHS of the first equation and on the LHS of the third equation. They are cancelled.

The equation that we obtain after the adding up and cancelling of the rearranged equations is exactly the one that we require.

So the calculated ΔH value of –84 kJ mol^{-1} is the required enthalpy change.

In Worked Example 10.1 above, all the equations were provided. Very often, however, the equations that we need to use are expressed in a problem in terms of recognised energy terms such as Enthalpy of Combustion, Formation, etc. (The full list of such terms and their definitions is given in Appendix 4 on pages 148–150.) Worked Example 10.2 below is an example of a problem expressed in these terms. The method of handling the problem is the same as before, although some of the detailed explanation given in Worked Example 10.1 is omitted.

WORKED EXAMPLE 10.2

Calculate the Enthalpy of Formation of methanol, CH_3OH, using the Enthalpies of Combustion of carbon, hydrogen and methanol obtained from Appendix 2, page 146.

The required equation for the Formation of methanol is written.

$$C\,(s) \quad + \quad 2H_2\,(g) \quad + \quad ^1/_2O_2\,(g) \quad \longrightarrow \quad CH_3OH\,(l)$$

The three combustion equations and their ΔH values, obtained from Appendix 2 are written and labelled as ①, ② and ③ for ease of reference.

①	$C\,(s)$	$+\ O_2\,(g)$	$\longrightarrow$	$CO_2\,(g)$	$\Delta H = -394$ kJ mol^{-1}
②	$H_2\,(g)$	$+\ ^1/_2O_2\,(g)$	$\longrightarrow$	$H_2O\,(l)$	$\Delta H = -286$ kJ mol^{-1}
③	$CH_3OH\,(l)$	$+\ 1^1/_2O_2\,(g)$	$\longrightarrow$	$CO_2\,(g) + 2H_2O\,(l)$	$\Delta H = -715$ kJ mol^{-1}

They are then rewritten below, multiplying and/or reversing them to suit the form of the required equation for the Formation of methanol. The ΔH values, multiplied and/or with changed signs where necessary, are written alongside.

①	$C\,(s)$	$+\ O_2\,(g)$	$\longrightarrow$	$CO_2\,(g)$	$\Delta H = -394$ kJ mol^{-1}
$2 \times$ ②	$2H_2\,(g)$	$+\ O_2\,(g)$	$\longrightarrow$	$2H_2O\,(l)$	$\Delta H = -572$ kJ mol^{-1}
$-$③	$CO_2\,(g)$	$+\ 2H_2O\,(l)$	$\longrightarrow$	$CH_3OH\,(l)\ +\ 1^1/_2O_2\,(g)$	$\Delta H = +715$ kJ mol^{-1}

The rearranged equations and their ΔH values can then be added up, after cancelling of species common to both sides (O_2 (g) and H_2O (l)), to give:

$$C\,(s) \quad + \quad 2H_2\,(g) \quad + \quad ^1/_2O_2\,(g) \quad \longrightarrow \quad CH_3OH\,(l) \qquad \Delta H = -251 \text{ kJ mol}^{-1}$$

This is the required equation and therefore the value for the Enthalpy of Formation of methanol is –251 kJ mol^{-1}.

Note that, in writing these equations, there was no choice in how to get C (s) on the LHS, $2H_2O$ (l) on the LHS and CH_3OH (l) on the RHS. However, if we had attempted to get $^1/_2O_2$ (g) on the LHS directly by selecting one equation, we would have had difficulty, since O_2 (g) appears in all three equations and we would not necessarily be sure which one(s) to use. The problem in this case was solved by ignoring it! If all three equations given can be written or rewritten to get the C (s), H_2O (l) and CH_3OH (l) in the right amounts and on the correct sides of the equation, then the O_2 (g), being the only remaining species, **must** work out correctly.

PROBLEMS 10.1 – 10.20

■ **In Problems 10.1 to 10.5, the required equations and ΔH values are given.**

■ **In Problems 10.6 to 10.20, equations will often require to be worked out and/or data obtained from Appendix 2 on page 146.**

10. 1 The equation for the combustion of methane, CH_4, is given below:

$$CH_4\,(g) \quad + \quad 2O_2\,(g) \quad \longrightarrow \quad CO_2\,(g) \quad + \quad 2H_2O\,(l)$$

Calculate the Enthalpy of Combustion of methane, using the data below.

$$C\,(s) \quad + \quad O_2\,(g) \quad \longrightarrow \quad CO_2\,(g) \qquad \Delta H = -394 \text{ kJ mol}^{-1}$$

$$H_2\,(g) \quad + \quad {}^1\!/_2O_2\,(g) \quad \longrightarrow \quad H_2O\,(l) \qquad \Delta H = -286 \text{ kJ mol}^{-1}$$

$$C\,(s) \quad + \quad 2H_2\,(g) \quad \longrightarrow \quad CH_4\,(g) \qquad \Delta H = \ -75 \text{ kJ mol}^{-1}$$

10. 2 The equation representing the combustion of ethane, C_2H_6, is given below:

$$C_2H_6\,(g) \quad + \quad 3{}^1\!/_2O_2\,(g) \quad \longrightarrow \quad 2CO_2\,(g) \quad + \quad 3H_2O\,(l)$$

Calculate the Enthalpy of Combustion of ethane, C_2H_6, using the Enthalpy of Formation of ethane and the Enthalpies of Combustion of carbon and hydrogen. The equations and ΔH values for these processes are given below:

$$2C\,(s) \quad + \quad 3H_2\,(g) \quad \longrightarrow \quad C_2H_6\,(g) \qquad \Delta H = \ -85 \text{ kJ mol}^{-1}$$

$$C\,(s) \quad + \quad O_2\,(g) \quad \longrightarrow \quad CO_2\,(g) \qquad \Delta H = -394 \text{ kJ mol}^{-1}$$

$$H_2\,(g) \quad + \quad {}^1\!/_2O_2\,(g) \quad \longrightarrow \quad H_2O\,(l) \qquad \Delta H = -286 \text{ kJ mol}^{-1}$$

10. 3 The Enthalpy of Formation of ethane, C_2H_6, is represented by the following equation:

$$2C\,(s) \quad + \quad 3H_2\,(g) \quad \longrightarrow \quad C_2H_6\,(g)$$

Calculate the Enthalpy of Formation of ethane using the Enthalpies of Combustion of hydrogen, carbon and ethane, represented by the equations and ΔH values below:

$$C\,(s) \quad + \quad O_2\,(g) \quad \longrightarrow \quad CO_2\,(g) \qquad \Delta H = \ -394 \text{ kJ mol}^{-1}$$

$$H_2\,(g) \quad + \quad {}^1\!/_2O_2\,(g) \quad \longrightarrow \quad H_2O\,(l) \qquad \Delta H = \ -286 \text{ kJ mol}^{-1}$$

$$C_2H_6\,(g) \quad + \quad 3{}^1\!/_2O_2\,(g) \quad \longrightarrow \quad 2CO_2\,(g) \quad + \quad 3H_2O\,(l) \quad \Delta H = -1542 \text{ kJ mol}^{-1}$$

10. 4 The Enthalpy of Combustion of propane, C_3H_8, is the ΔH for the following reaction:

$$C_3H_8 \quad + \quad 5O_2\,(g) \quad \longrightarrow \quad 3CO_2\,(g) \quad + \quad 4H_2O\,(l)$$

Calculate the Enthalpy of Combustion of propane using the Enthalpy of Formation of propane and the Enthalpies of Combustion of carbon and hydrogen. The equations and ΔH values for these processes are given below:

$$3C\,(s) \quad + \quad 4H_2\,(g) \quad \longrightarrow \quad C_3H_8\,(g) \qquad \Delta H = -104 \text{ kJ mol}^{-1}$$

$$C\,(s) \quad + \quad O_2\,(g) \quad \longrightarrow \quad CO_2\,(g) \qquad \Delta H = -394 \text{ kJ mol}^{-1}$$

$$H_2\,(g) \quad + \quad {}^1\!/_2O_2\,(g) \quad \longrightarrow \quad H_2O\,(l) \qquad \Delta H = -286 \text{ kJ mol}^{-1}$$

10. 5   The formation of butane, C_4H_{10}, is represented by the equation below:

$$4C\,(s)\quad +\quad 5H_2\,(g)\quad \longrightarrow\quad C_4H_{10}\,(g)$$

Calculate the Enthalpy of Formation of butane using the Enthalpies of Combustion of butane, hydrogen and carbon represented by the equations and ΔH values below:

$$C_4H_{10}\,(g)\quad +\quad 6\tfrac{1}{2}O_2\,(g)\quad \longrightarrow\quad 4CO_2\,(g)\quad +\quad 5H_2O\,(l)\qquad \Delta H = -2877 \text{ kJ mol}^{-1}$$

$$H_2\,(g)\quad +\quad \tfrac{1}{2}O_2\,(g)\quad \longrightarrow\quad H_2O\,(l)\qquad \Delta H = -286 \text{ kJ mol}^{-1}$$

$$C\,(s)\quad +\quad O_2\,(g)\quad \longrightarrow\quad CO_2\,(g)\qquad \Delta H = -394 \text{ kJ mol}^{-1}$$

10. 6   Calculate the Enthalpy of Combustion of ethanol, C_2H_5OH, using the Enthalpies of Combustion of carbon and hydrogen and the Enthalpy of Formation of ethanol.
(**Note:** Don't forget to count the oxygen present in ethanol when balancing the combustion equation!)

10. 7   Calculate the Enthalpy of Formation of ethanoic acid, CH_3COOH, using the Enthalpies of Combustion of ethanoic acid, carbon and hydrogen.

10. 8   Calculate the Enthalpy of Formation of propan-1-ol, C_3H_7OH, using the Enthalpies of Combustion of propan-1-ol, carbon and hydrogen.

10. 9   Calculate the Enthalpy of Combustion of benzene, C_6H_6, using the Enthalpy of Formation of benzene and the Enthalpies of Combustion of carbon and hydrogen.

10.10   Calculate the Enthalpy of Formation of ethyne, C_2H_2, using the Enthalpies of Combustion of ethyne, hydrogen and carbon.

10.11   Calculate the Enthalpy of Formation of methanoic acid, $HCOOH$, using the Enthalpies of Combustion of methanoic acid, carbon and hydrogen.

10.12   The reaction of ethanol with oxygen to form ethanoic acid and water is represented by the equation below:

$$C_2H_5OH\,(l)\quad +\quad O_2\,(g)\quad \longrightarrow\quad CH_3COOH\,(l)\quad +\quad H_2O\,(l)$$

Use the Enthalpies of Combustion of ethanol and ethanoic acid to calculate the ΔH for the above reaction.

10.13   The equation below represents the hydrogenation of ethene to ethane:

$$C_2H_4\,(g)\quad +\quad H_2\,(g)\quad \longrightarrow\quad C_2H_6\,(g)$$

Use the Enthalpies of Combustion of ethene, hydrogen and ethane to calculate the ΔH for the above reaction.

10.14   The fermentation of glucose, $C_6H_{12}O_6$, to ethanol and carbon dioxide can be represented by the equation below:

$$C_6H_{12}O_6\,(s)\quad \longrightarrow\quad 2C_2H_5OH\,(l)\quad +\quad 2CO_2\,(g)$$

Calculate the ΔH for this reaction using the Enthalpies of Combustion of ethanol and glucose. (The Enthalpy of Combustion of glucose is -2813 kJ mol^{-1}.)

10.15   Use the Enthalpies of Combustion of ethyne, (C_2H_2), ethane, (C_2H_6), and hydrogen to calculate the ΔH for the complete hydrogenation of ethyne given by the equation below:

$$C_2H_2\,(g)\quad +\quad 2H_2\,(g)\quad \longrightarrow\quad C_2H_6\,(g)$$

10.16 The Enthalpy of Formation of diborane, B_2H_6, is the ΔH for the following reaction:

$$2B\,(s) \quad + \quad 3H_2\,(g) \longrightarrow \quad B_2H_6\,(g)$$

Calculate the Enthalpy of Formation of diborane using the Enthalpy of Combustion of hydrogen and the equations and ΔH values for the Enthalpy of Formation of boron oxide and the Enthalpy of Combustion of diborane noted below:

$$2B\,(s) \quad + \quad 1^{1}/_{2}O_2\,(g) \longrightarrow \quad B_2O_3\,(s) \qquad\qquad \Delta H = \ -612\ \text{kJ mol}^{-1}$$

$$B_2H_6\,(g) \quad + \quad 3O_2\,(g) \longrightarrow \quad B_2O_3\,(s) \quad + \quad 3H_2O\,(l) \qquad \Delta H = \ -1058\ \text{kJ mol}^{-1}$$

10.17 Use the Enthalpies of Combustion of methane, hydrogen and ethyne, C_2H_2, to obtain the ΔH for the reaction represented by the equation below.

$$2CH_4\,(g) \longrightarrow \quad C_2H_2\,(g) \quad + \quad 3H_2\,(g)$$

10.18

$$Na\,(s) \quad + \quad {}^{1}/_{2}Cl_2\,(g) \longrightarrow \quad Na^+\,(g) \quad + \quad Cl^-\,(g) \qquad \Delta H = \ +365\ \text{kJ mol}^{-1}$$

$$Na\,(s) \quad + \quad {}^{1}/_{2}Cl_2\,(g) \longrightarrow \quad Na^+Cl^-(s) \qquad\qquad\qquad \Delta H = \ -411\ \text{kJ mol}^{-1}$$

Use the above information to calculate the ΔH for the reaction below:

$$Na^+Cl^-\,(s) \longrightarrow \quad Na^+\,(g) \quad + \quad Cl^-\,(g)$$

10.19

$$Cu\,(s) \longrightarrow \quad Cu^{2+}\,(aq) \quad + \quad 2e^- \qquad\qquad \Delta H = \ +795\ \text{kJ mol}^{-1}$$

$$Cu\,(s) \longrightarrow \quad Cu^+\,(aq) \quad + \quad e^- \qquad\qquad\quad \Delta H = \ +602\ \text{kJ mol}^{-1}$$

Use the above information to calculate the ΔH for the reaction below:

$$2Cu^+\,(aq) \longrightarrow \quad Cu^{2+}\,(aq) \quad + \quad Cu\,(s)$$

10.20 The Enthalpies of Formation of methylhydrazine, CH_3NHNH_2, and dinitrogen tetroxide, N_2O_4 are $+53$ kJ mol^{-1} and -20 kJ mol^{-1} respectively. Use this information and the Enthalpies of Combustion of carbon and hydrogen to obtain the ΔH for the reaction described by the equation below:

$$4CH_3NHNH_2 \quad + \quad 5N_2O_4 \longrightarrow \quad 4CO_2 \quad + \quad 12H_2O \quad + \quad 9N_2$$

11. HESS'S LAW USING BOND ENTHALPIES

In chemical reactions, the bonds within the reactant molecules are broken and then new bonds are made as the products are formed. For example, consider the burning of hydrogen gas in oxygen represented by the equation below:

$$2H_2 \ + \ O_2 \ \longrightarrow \ 2H_2O$$

This reaction can be considered by means of the diagrams below.

Energy put in to break
the bonds within the
hydrogen and oxygen molecules

Energy given out
as the bonds within the
water molecules are made

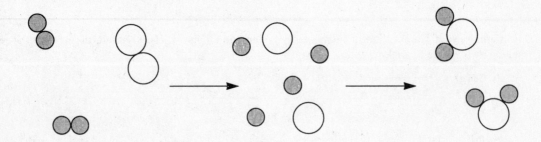

- In this reaction, more energy is given out in making the new bonds than is put in to break the bonds of the reactants. So, *overall*, energy is given out in the form of heat as the reaction takes place; this is called an **exothermic** reaction. The heat given out causes the surroundings (air, container, etc.) to increase in temperature.

- In the *opposite* type of reaction, more energy needs to be put in to break the bonds of the reactants than is given out when the new bonds in the products are made. So, *overall*, energy is taken in as the reaction takes place; this is called an **endothermic** reaction. The heat energy is taken from the surroundings, causing a drop in temperature.

It is possible to calculate numerical values for the amount of energy involved in the making and breaking of chemical bonds. For example, to break the bonds in 1 mol of N_2 gas requires an input of 949 kJ of energy. To break the bonds in 1 mol of F_2 gas needs only 155 kJ. These values are known as the **bond enthalpies** of the particular bonds:

Bond	Bond Enthalpy (kJ mol^{-1})
N $\equiv$ N	949
F – F	155

Appendix 2 on page 146, has a table listing the bond enthalpies of all the common covalent bonds we shall come across. It should be noted that some of them are described as **mean** bond enthalpies. "Mean" in this sense means "average" and refers to the fact that some bonds are present in several different compounds; the values in the table are the averages of the enthalpies of these bonds in these different compounds. For example, the C–H bond appears in many different compounds such as alkanes, alkenes, alcohols, etc. The quoted value for the C–H bond enthalpy of 414 kJ mol^{-1} is an average value measured over all these different types of compound.

On the same page as the table of Bond Enthalpies is a box entitled Enthalpy of Sublimation of Carbon, described by the equation:

$$C\,(s) \longrightarrow C\,(g) \qquad \Delta H = +715 \text{ kJ}$$

This refers to the energy needed to be put in to break completely all the bonds in 1 mole of solid carbon, turning it into 1 mole of carbon in the gas state.

Hess's Law of thermochemistry tells us that the ΔH for a reaction depends only on the nature of the reactants and the products and **not** on how the reaction is carried out. This means that the ΔH calculated by breaking all the bonds of the reactants and then reforming them to make the bonds of the products is the same as the ΔH obtained from carrying out the reaction directly. This principle means that we can calculate enthalpy changes from bond enthalpy and sublimation enthalpy data as shown in the following Worked Examples.

WORKED EXAMPLE 11.1

Calculate the enthalpy change (ΔH) for the burning of hydrogen, as represented by the equation below, using bond enthalpy data.

$$2H_2 \text{ (g)} \quad + \quad O_2 \text{ (g)} \quad \longrightarrow \quad 2H_2O \text{ (g)}$$

With reference to the table of Bond Enthalpies on page 146, we set out the calculation as below.

Bond Breaking (energy put in)			Bond Making (energy given out)		
2 mol of H — H = 2 × 436 =	872 kJ		4 mol of O — H = 4 × 458 =	1832 kJ	
1 mol of O = O =	497 kJ				
Total energy put in:	+1369 kJ		Total energy given out	−1832 kJ	

The energy put in has been given a positive sign (+) to show that this energy is being added to the reactants; the energy given out is given a negative sign (−) to show that it is being lost as the products are formed.

We can obtain the ΔH for this reaction by simply adding the "Energy put in" and "Energy given out" figures, while remembering that the latter figure is a negative quantity.

$$
\begin{aligned}
\text{Overall enthalpy (energy) change } (\Delta H) \quad &= \quad 1369 + (-1832) \text{ kJ} \\
&= \quad 1369 - 1832 \text{ kJ} \\
&= \quad \mathbf{-463\ kJ}
\end{aligned}
$$

Note that the value of 463 kJ of heat being given out referred to the burning of two moles of H_2 as expressed in the original equation. If we required the quantity of heat given out when one mole of H_2 is burned, we would need to halve the value calculated above.

WORKED EXAMPLE 11.2

Calculate the Enthalpy of Formation of chloroethane, C_2H_5Cl, using Bond Enthalpy data and the Enthalpy of Sublimation of carbon (Appendix 2, page 146).

As with the previous example, the first step is to write the required equation, in this case, for the Formation of chloroethane. This is defined (see Appendix 4 on pages 148–150 for this and other definitions of enthalpy terms) as the formation of 1 mol of the substance from its elements in their room temperature states. So the equation is:

$$2C \text{ (s)} \quad + \quad 2\tfrac{1}{2}H_2 \text{ (g)} \quad + \quad 1/2Cl_2 \text{ (g)} \quad \longrightarrow \quad C_2H_5Cl \text{ (g)}$$

The data can be set out in the form of a table as shown below. However, before doing so, it is useful to draw the extended structural formula of chloroethane, to help us avoid missing out any of its bonds in the calculation.

$$
\begin{array}{ccc}
 & H & H \\
 & | & | \\
H - & C - & C - Cl \\
 & | & | \\
 & H & H
\end{array}
\qquad \text{Chlorethane}
$$

Bond Breaking (energy put in)			Bond Making (energy given out)		
2 mol of C (s)	= 2 × 715* =	1430 kJ	1 mol of C — C	=	337 kJ
2½ mol of H — H	= 2½ × 436 =	1090 kJ	1 mol of C — Cl	=	326 kJ
½ mol of Cl — Cl	= ½ × 243 =	121·5 kJ	5 mol of C — H = 5 × 414 =		2070 kJ
Total energy put in:	=	+2641·5 kJ	Total energy given out	=	−2733 kJ

$$\Delta H \text{ for reaction} = +2641 \cdot 5 + (-2733) \text{ kJ mol}^{-1}$$
$$= 2641 \cdot 5 - 2733 \quad \text{kJ mol}^{-1}$$
$$= \mathbf{-91 \cdot 5 \text{ kJ mol}^{-1}}$$

* Note that the enthalpy value starred in the table is the Enthalpy of Sublimation of Carbon, since we are breaking solid carbon into gaseous carbon atoms; this term must not be confused with the Bond Enthalpy for C — C which refers to the carbon-carbon bond in organic compounds.

PROBLEMS 11.1 – 11.20

Problems 11.1 to 11.20 are of the type shown in Worked Examples 11.1 and 11.2. In Problems 11.1 to 11.10 the required chemical equation is supplied; in some of the later problems the starting equation needs to be worked out first.

11. 1 Use Bond Enthalpy data to calculate the ΔH for the reaction below.

$$2F_2 \text{ (g)} \quad + \quad 2H_2O \text{ (g)} \quad \longrightarrow \quad 4HF \text{ (g)} \quad + \quad O_2 \text{ (g)}$$

11. 2 Use Bond Enthalpy data to calculate the ΔH for the reaction below.

$$CH_4 \text{ (g)} \quad + \quad 2O_2 \text{ (g)} \quad \longrightarrow \quad CO_2 \text{ (g)} \quad + \quad 2H_2O \text{ (g)}$$

11. 3 Use Bond Enthalpy data to calculate the ΔH for the complete hydrogenation of 1 mole of ethene ($H_2C = CH_2$) to ethane according to the following equation.

$$C_2H_4 \text{ (g)} \quad + \quad H_2 \text{ (g)} \quad \longrightarrow \quad C_2H_6 \text{ (g)}$$

11. 4 Use Bond Enthalpy data to calculate the ΔH for the reaction below.

$$CH_4 \text{ (g)} \quad + \quad Cl_2 \text{ (g)} \quad \longrightarrow \quad CH_3Cl \text{ (g)} \quad + \quad HCl \text{ (g)}$$

11. 5 Use Bond Enthalpy data to calculate the ΔH for the reaction below.

$$C_2H_4 \text{ (g)} \quad + \quad H_2O \text{ (g)} \quad \longrightarrow \quad C_2H_5OH \text{ (g)}$$

11. 6 Calculate the ΔH for the chlorination of ethene ($H_2C = CH_2$) which is represented by the following equation:

$$C_2H_4 \text{ (g)} \quad + \quad Cl_2 \text{ (g)} \quad \longrightarrow \quad CH_2ClCH_2Cl \text{ (g)}$$

11. 7 Use Bond Enthalpy data and the Enthalpy of Sublimation of carbon to calculate the Enthalpy of Formation of methane, CH_4 (g), as represented by the equation below.

$$C \text{ (s)} \quad + \quad 2H_2 \text{ (g)} \quad \longrightarrow \quad CH_4 \text{ (g)}$$

11. 8 Use Bond Enthalpy data and the Enthalpy of Sublimation of carbon to calculate the Enthalpy of Formation of propene gas, C_3H_6 (g), as represented by the equation below

$$3C \text{ (s)} \quad + \quad 3H_2 \text{ (g)} \quad \longrightarrow \quad C_3H_6 \text{ (g)}$$

11. 9 Calculate the Enthalpy of Formation of tetrafluoromethane, CF_4 (g), using Bond Enthalpy data and the Enthalpy of Sublimation of carbon. The Formation of tetrafluoromethane is described by the equation below.

$$C \text{ (s)} \quad + \quad 2F_2 \text{ (g)} \quad \longrightarrow \quad CF_4 \text{ (g)}$$

11.10 Use Bond Enthalpy data to calculate the ΔH for the fluorination of ethene ($H_2C = CH_2$) shown by the equation below.

$$C_2H_4 \text{ (g)} \quad + \quad F_2 \text{ (g)} \quad \longrightarrow \quad C_2H_4F_2 \text{ (g)}$$

11.11 Use Bond Enthalpy data and the Enthalpy of Sublimation of carbon to calculate the Enthalpy of Formation of butene gas, C_4H_8 (g).

11.12 Calculate the enthalpy change (ΔH) for the formation of CCl_3F (g) shown by the equation below, using Bond Enthalpy data and the Enthalpy of Sublimation of carbon.

$$C \text{ (s)} \quad + \quad 1^1/_2Cl_2 \text{ (g)} \quad + \quad ^1/_2F_2 \text{ (g)} \quad \longrightarrow \quad CCl_3F \text{ (g)}$$

11.13 Calculate the Enthalpy of Formation of ethyne ($H - C \equiv C - H$) using the Enthalpy of Sublimation of carbon and Bond Enthalpy data.

11.14 The hydration of ethyne, C_2H_2 (g), to ethanal, CH_3CHO (g), can be represented by the equation below which shows partial structural formulae. Calculate the ΔH for the reaction.

$$H - C \equiv C - H \text{ (g)} + \quad H_2O \text{ (g)} \quad \longrightarrow \quad CH_3C\underset{H}{\overset{O}{\big\langle}} \text{ (g)}$$

11.15 Calculate the ΔH for the reaction described by the equation below using the Enthalpy of Sublimation of carbon and Bond Enthalpy data.

$$2C \text{ (s)} \quad + \quad 1^1/_2Cl_2 \text{ (g)} \quad + \quad 1^1/_2F_2 \text{ (g)} \quad \longrightarrow \quad CCl_3CF_3 \text{ (g)}$$

11.16 Calculate the ΔH for the reaction below using Bond Enthalpy data.

$$C_2H_6 \text{ (g)} \quad + \quad 3^1/_2O_2 \text{ (g)} \quad \longrightarrow \quad 2CO_2 \text{ (g)} \quad + \quad 3H_2O \text{ (g)}$$

11.17 The Enthalpy of Sublimation of phosphorus is 315 kJ mol^{-1} and the P — H Bond Enthalpy is 320 kJ mol^{-1}. Use this and other Bond Enthalpy information to calculate the Enthalpy of Formation of phosphine, PH_3 (g).

11.18 The Enthalpy of Sublimation of silicon is 439 kJ mol^{-1} and the Bond Enthalpy of Si — H is 318 kJ mol^{-1}. Use this and other Bond Enthalpies information to calculate the ΔH for the reaction below.

$$Si_2H_6 \text{ (g)} \quad \longrightarrow \quad 2Si \text{ (s)} \quad + \quad 3H_2 \text{ (g)}$$

(**Note:** In this case, the bonds in solid silicon, Si (s), are being made from gaseous silicon, Si (g), after all the bonds in Si_2H_6 (g) have been broken. This process is therefore the reverse of the sublimation of silicon.)

11.19 The Enthalpy of Sublimation of sulphur is 220 kJ mol^{-1} and the S — H Bond Enthalpy is 338 kJ mol^{-1}. Use this and other Bond Enthalpy information to calculate the Enthalpy of Formation of hydrogen sulphide, H_2S (g).

11.20 Use Bond Enthalpy data to calculate the ΔH for the chlorination of ethanal to trichloroethanal shown by the equation below.

$$CH_3C\underset{H}{\overset{O}{\big\langle}} \text{ (g)} \quad + \quad 3Cl_2 \text{ (g)} \quad \longrightarrow \quad CCl_3C\underset{H}{\overset{O}{\big\langle}} \text{ (g)} \quad + \quad 3HCl \text{ (g)}$$

12. USING ENTHALPY DIAGRAMS

Consider three imaginary chemical reactions and their ΔH values as shown below.

$$
\begin{array}{llll}
A \longrightarrow B & \Delta H1 & = & +40 \text{ kJ mol}^{-1} \\
B \longrightarrow C & \Delta H2 & = & -30 \text{ kJ mol}^{-1} \\
C \longrightarrow D & \Delta H3 & = & -20 \text{ kJ mol}^{-1}
\end{array}
$$

We can plot the enthalpy changes for these reactions on the enthalpy diagram below. Note that the actual enthalpy values of the substances are not labelled on the axis because they are not as important as the enthalpy changes which are shown beside the arrows indicating the direction of the reactions.

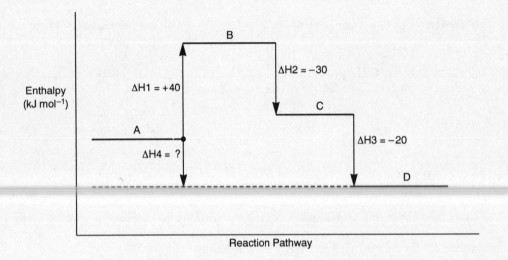

The information in the diagram can be used to calculate the enthalpy change, ΔH4, for the reaction:

$$ A \longrightarrow D $$

There are two ways in which ΔH4 can be obtained from the diagram. These are described as follows.

METHOD 1

Ignoring for the moment the directions of the arrows and the positive and negative signs, we can say that:

The "distance" represented by ΔH4 is the "distance" from B to D less the distance from B to A.

The "distance" from B to D is $30 + 20 = 50$ kJ mol^{-1} and that from B to A is 40 kJ mol^{-1}, so the "distance" from A to D must be $50 - 40 = 10$ kJ mol^{-1}.

Since the enthalpy change from A to D involves going **down** the diagram, this represents a **decrease** in enthalpy and so has a negative sign.

That is, the ΔH for the reaction A ⟶ D is −10 kJ mol⁻¹

METHOD 2

The enthalpy change $\Delta H4$ can be achieved by starting at A and carrying out the following steps:

A	⟶	B	$\Delta H1$	=	$+40$ kJ mol^{-1}	followed by
B	⟶	C	$\Delta H2$	=	-30 kJ mol^{-1}	followed by
C	⟶	D	$\Delta H3$	=	-20 kJ mol^{-1}	

This means that:

$$
\begin{aligned}
\Delta H4 &= \Delta H1 + \Delta H2 + \Delta H3 \\
&= 40 + (-30) + (-20) \\
&= 40 - 30 - 20 \\
&= \mathbf{-10 \ kJ \ mol^{-1}}
\end{aligned}
$$

Method 1 and Method 2 are essentially the same, although some students may find Method 1 simpler to handle because it does not require manipulation of negative numbers. However, Method 1 is really only practicable when an energy diagram showing the direction of the change is provided.

Enthalpy diagrams are often used to illustrate the different enthalpy changes involved in processes such as the formation of ionic compounds and the dissolving of ionic compounds in water. The use of enthalpy diagrams in these processes can be seen in the Worked Examples next.

WORKED EXAMPLE 12.1

Consider the energy diagram below which shows the energy steps relating to the formation of sodium chloride, Na^+Cl^- (s) from its elements.

The Enthalpy of formation of sodium chloride, marked ΔH6 on the diagram, relates to the equation:

$$Na \text{ (s)} \quad + \quad \tfrac{1}{2}Cl_2 \text{ (g)} \quad \longrightarrow \quad Na^+Cl^- \text{ (s)}$$

Calculate the value for ΔH6 using the data given. (All enthalpy changes shown are in units of kJ mol^{-1}.)

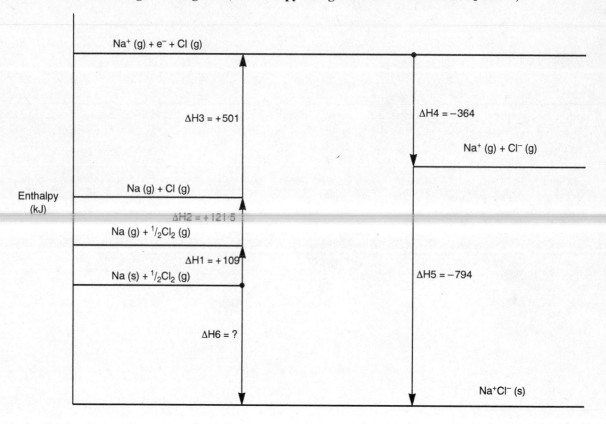

The names of the enthalpy changes shown on the diagram are noted below. The definitions of these and other enthalpy terms are given in the Appendix.

ΔH1	=	Enthalpy of Sublimation of Na
ΔH2	=	$\tfrac{1}{2}$ × Bond Enthalpy of Cl — Cl
ΔH3	=	1st Ionisation Enthalpy of Na
ΔH4	=	Electron Gain Enthalpy of Cl
ΔH5	=	Lattice Making Enthalpy of NaCl

Data relating to Bond Enthalpies and Ionisation Enthalpies are on pages 146 and 147 respectively.

The calculation of ΔH6 can be done by the "distance" method (Method 1) or by the more mathematical approach (Method 2), both described for the simple example given in the introduction to this chapter.

METHOD 1

Ignoring, just for now, all signs indicating directions of enthalpy changes, we can see from the diagram that:

The "distance" $\Delta H6$ is the same as the total of the "distances" $\Delta H4$ and $\Delta H5$ less the total of the "distances" $\Delta H1$, $\Delta H2$ and $\Delta H3$.

The "distance" $\Delta H4 + \Delta H5$	$= \quad 364 + 794$	$= \quad 1158 \ \text{kJ mol}^{-1}$
The "distance" $\Delta H1 + \Delta H2 + \Delta H3$	$= \quad 109 + 121 \cdot 5 + 501$	$= \quad 731 \cdot 5 \ \text{kJ mol}^{-1}$
So the "distance" $\Delta H6$	$= \quad 1158 - 731 \cdot 5$	$= \quad 426 \cdot 5 \ \text{kJ mol}^{-1}$

This calculated "distance" is the **positive value** of the enthalpy change $\Delta H6$; however, the **direction** of the change is important. From the diagram, it can be seen that the arrow describing $\Delta H6$ is pointing **downwards**; that is, the process has a **negative** enthalpy change.

So $\Delta H6 = -426 \cdot 5 \ \text{kJ mol}^{-1}$

METHOD 2

From the energy diagram, the Formation of Na^+Cl^- (s) represented by $\Delta H6$ can be obtained by following the route $\Delta H1$, $\Delta H2$, $\Delta H3$, $\Delta H4$ and finally $\Delta H5$.

So
$$
\begin{aligned}
\Delta H6 &= \Delta H1 + \Delta H2 + \Delta H3 + \Delta H4 + \Delta H5 \\
&= 109 + 121 \cdot 5 + 501 + (-364) + (-794) \\
&= 109 + 121 \cdot 5 + 501 - 364 - 794 \\
&= \mathbf{-426 \cdot 5 \ kJ \ mol^{-1}}
\end{aligned}
$$

It is worthwhile practice to take a **different** set of five of the above ΔH values and confirm the sixth value by calculation.

WORKED EXAMPLE 12.2

Consider the energy diagram below which shows the various energy steps involved in the formation of lithium chloride. The values of some enthalpy changes, in kJ mol^{-1}, are given on the diagram. The diagram is *not* drawn to scale. Use the data given to calculate ΔH1, the Enthalpy of Sublimation of lithium.

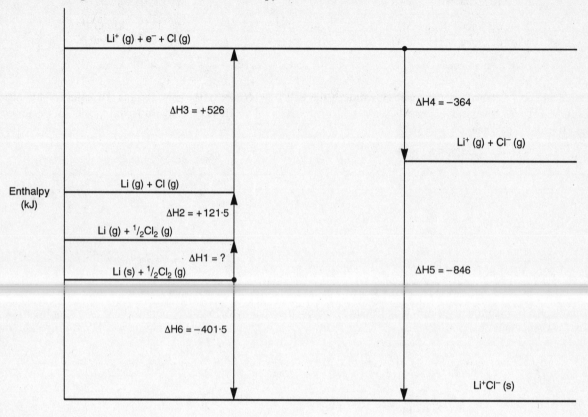

Method 1

The "distance" represented by ΔH1 is the total "distance" of ΔH4 and ΔH5 less the total "distance" of ΔH3, ΔH2 and ΔH6, ignoring the signs indicating the directions of these processes.

The "distance" of ΔH4 and ΔH5   =   364 + 846   =   1210 kJ mol^{-1}
The "distance" of ΔH3, ΔH2 and ΔH6 =   526 + 121·5 + 401·5 =   1049 kJ mol^{-1}

So the "distance" of ΔH1 = 1210 − 1049 = 161 kJ mol^{-1}

ΔH1 is a positive enthalpy change, as represented by the upward arrow on the diagram.

So ΔH1 = + 161 kJ mol^{-1}

Method 2

$\Delta H1$ can be achieved by carrying out the following steps in order:

	$\Delta H6$	followed by
the **opposite** of	$\Delta H5$	followed by
the **opposite** of	$\Delta H4$	followed by
the **opposite** of	$\Delta H3$	followed by
the **opposite** of	$\Delta H2$	

That is

$$
\begin{aligned}
\Delta H1 &= \Delta H6 - \Delta H5 - \Delta H4 - \Delta H3 - \Delta H2 \\
&= (-401\cdot5) - (-846) - (-364) - (+526) - (+121\cdot5) \\
&= -401\cdot5 + 846 + 364 - 526 - 121\cdot5 \\
&= \mathbf{+161 \ kJ \ mol^{-1}}
\end{aligned}
$$

It will be obvious that the use of Method 2 in this particular example requires considerable care to prevent error!

WORKED EXAMPLE 12.3

The Enthalpy of Solution of potassium fluoride is represented by the following equation and is labelled $\Delta H4$ on the energy diagram below.

$$K^+ F^- (s) \longrightarrow K^+(aq) + F^-(aq)$$

Calculate the value for the Enthalpy of Solution of potassium fluoride using the diagram and data given below.

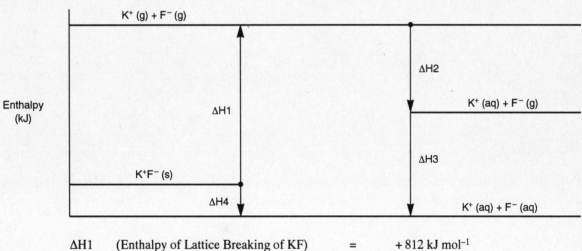

$\Delta H1$	(Enthalpy of Lattice Breaking of KF)	=	$+ 812$ kJ mol^{-1}
$\Delta H2$	(Hydration Enthalpy K$^+$)	=	$- 323$ kJ mol^{-1}
$\Delta H3$	(Hydration Enthalpy F$^-$)	=	$- 507$ kJ mol^{-1}

Method 1

The "distance" represented by $\Delta H4$ is the same as the total "distance" of $\Delta H2$ and $\Delta H3$ less the "distance" of $\Delta H1$.

So the "distance" of $\Delta H4$ = 323 + 507 – 812

= 18 kJ mol^{-1}

But since $\Delta H4$ is shown by a downward arrow, indicating a negative enthalpy change, we conclude that

$$\Delta H4 \;=\; -18 \text{ kJ mol}^{-1}$$

Method 2

The enthalpy step $\Delta H4$ can be obtained by carrying out $\Delta H1$, $\Delta H2$ and then $\Delta H3$. That is:

$$
\begin{aligned}
\Delta H4 &= \Delta H1 + \Delta H2 + \Delta H3 \\
&= 812 + (-323) + (-507) \\
&= 812 - 323 - 507 \\
&= -18 \text{ kJ mol}^{-1}
\end{aligned}
$$

PROBLEMS 12.1 to 12.10

The following problems are of the types shown in Worked Examples 12.1, 12.2 and 12.3.

12. 1 Consider the energy diagram below which shows the various energy steps involved in the formation of potassium chloride. The values of some enthalpy changes, in kJ mol^{-1}, are given on the diagram. The diagram is **not** drawn to scale.

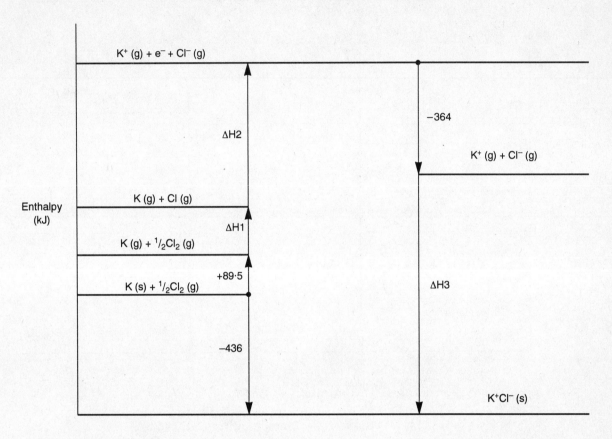

(a) Name the enthalpy terms for the changes shown on the diagram above, with ΔH values of $+89\cdot5$ kJ mol^{-1} and -364 kJ mol^{-1} respectively.

(b) Obtain values for $\Delta H1$ and $\Delta H2$ from pages 146 and 147 respectively.

(c) Use your answers to (b) and the information on the diagram to calculate the value for $\Delta H3$.

12. 2 Consider the energy diagram below which shows the various energy steps involved in the formation of rubidium fluoride. The values of some enthalpy changes, in kJ mol^{-1}, are given on the diagram. The diagram is **not** drawn to scale.

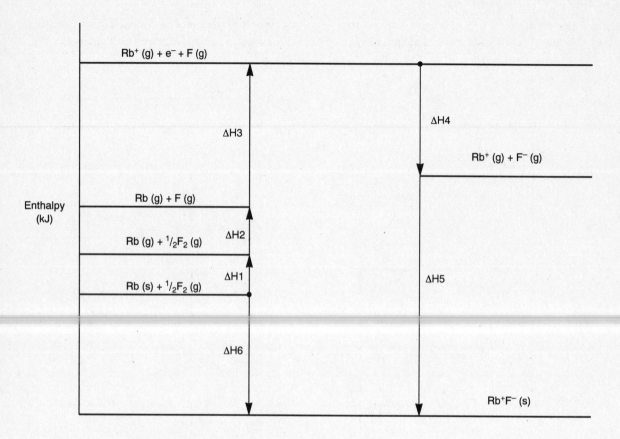

(a)   Name the enthalpy terms labelled $\Delta H1$ to $\Delta H6$.

(b)   Refer to pages 146 and 147 to obtain values for the enthalpy steps $\Delta H2$ and $\Delta H3$.

(c)   Use the above information, and that below, to calculate the value for $\Delta H6$.

$$\Delta H1 \;\; = \;\; +86 \;\; \text{kJ mol}^{-1}$$
$$\Delta H4 \;\; = \;\; -332 \;\; \text{kJ mol}^{-1}$$
$$\Delta H5 \;\; = \;\; -775 \;\; \text{kJ mol}^{-1}$$

12. 3 Consider the energy diagram below which shows the various energy steps involved in the formation of lithium fluoride. The values of some enthalpy changes, in kJ mol^{-1}, are given on the diagram. The diagram is **not** drawn to scale.

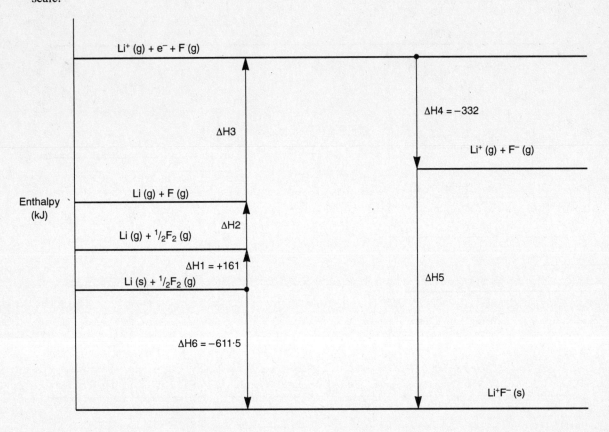

(a) Name the enthalpy changes $\Delta H1$ to $\Delta H6$.

(b) Obtain values for $\Delta H2$ and $\Delta H3$ from pages 146 and 147.

(c) Use the data on the diagram, and that obtained in part *(b)*, to calculate $\Delta H5$.

12. 4 The enthalpy diagram below, which is **not** drawn to scale, represents the enthalpy steps involved in the formation of magnesium chloride.

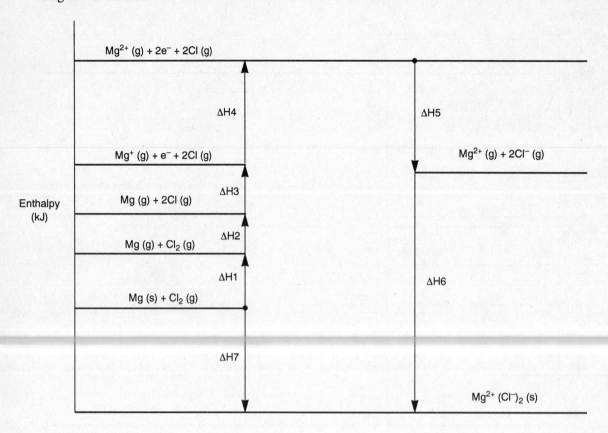

(a)   Name the enthalpy changes $\Delta H1$ to $\Delta H7$.

(b)   Obtain the values for $\Delta H2$, $\Delta H3$ and $\Delta H4$ from pages 146 and 147.

(c)   Calculate the value for $\Delta H1$ using your answers to *(b)* and the data given below.

$$\Delta H5 = -728 \text{ kJ mol}^{-1}$$
$$\Delta H6 = -2489 \text{ kJ mol}^{-1}$$
$$\Delta H7 = -642 \text{ kJ mol}^{-1}$$

12. 5 The enthalpy diagram below, which is **not** drawn to scale, represents the enthalpy steps involved in the formation of calcium chloride. The values of some enthalpy changes, in kJ mol^{-1}, are given on the diagram.

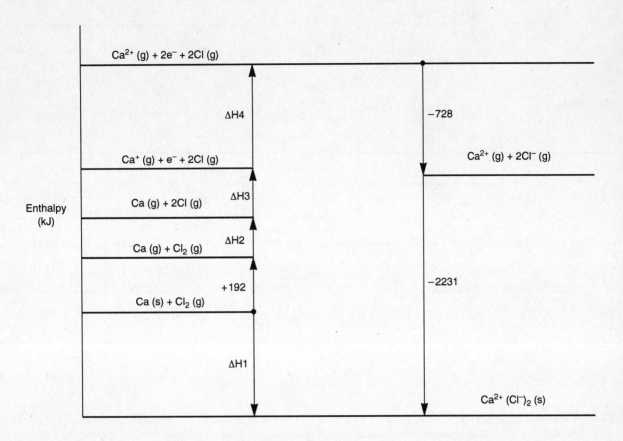

(a)   Obtain values for ΔH2, ΔH3 and ΔH4 from pages 146 and 147.

(b)   Using the data obtained at *(a)*, and that given on the diagram, calculate the value for ΔH1.

12. 6 The enthalpy diagram below shows the energy steps involved in the formation of a solution of lithium chloride. The values of some enthalpy changes, in kJ mol^{-1}, are given on the diagram. The diagram is **not** drawn to scale.

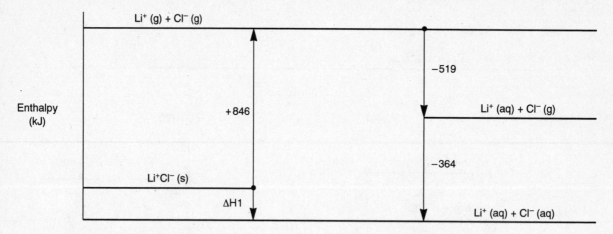

(a)   Name the enthalpy changes shown above, with values +846, −519 and −364 kJ mol^{-1} respectively.

(b)   Name, and calculate the value of, enthalpy change ΔH1.

12. 7 The enthalpy diagram below shows the energy steps involved in the formation of a solution of sodium bromide. The values of some enthalpy changes, in kJ mol^{-1}, are given on the diagram. The diagram is **not** drawn to scale.

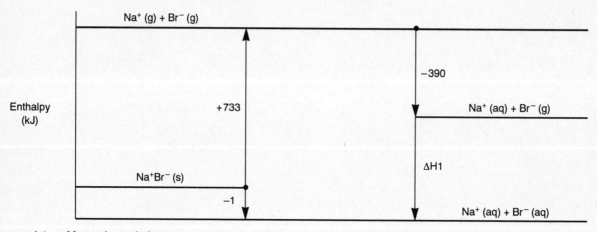

(a)   Name the enthalpy terms represented by the ΔH values +733, −390 and −1 kJ mol^{-1} respectively.

(b)   Name, and calculate the value of, the enthalpy change represented by ΔH1.

12. 8 The enthalpy diagram below shows the energy steps involved in the formation of a solution of potassium bromide. The values of some enthalpy changes, in kJ mol^{-1}, are given on the diagram. The diagram is **not** drawn to scale.

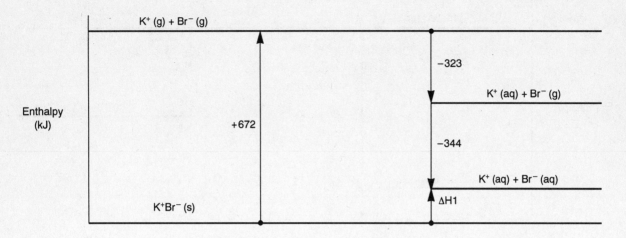

(a)   Name the enthalpy steps with values +672, −323 and −344 kJ mol^{-1} shown on the diagram above.

(b)   Name, and calculate the value of, the enthalpy change labelled ΔH1.

12. 9 The enthalpy diagram below shows the energy steps involved in the formation of a solution of calcium chloride. The diagram is **not** drawn to scale.

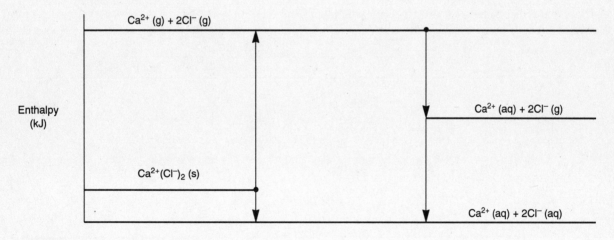

Calculate the Enthalpy of Hydration of Ca^{2+}, with the aid of the above diagram, and given the following data.

Lattice Breaking Enthalpy of calcium chloride   =   +2231 kJ mol^{-1}
Hydration Enthalpy of Cl$^-$ =   −364 kJ mol^{-1}
Enthalpy of Solution of calcium chloride   =   −83 kJ mol^{-1}

12.10 The enthalpy diagram below shows the energy steps involved in the formation of a solution of strontium chloride. The diagram is **not** drawn to scale.

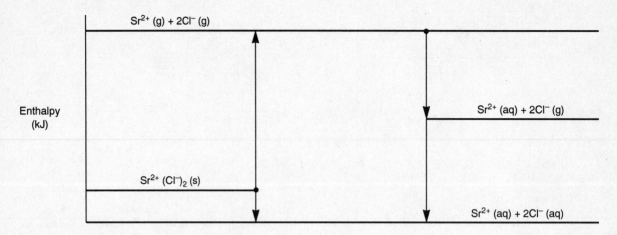

Calculate the Enthalpy of Solution of strontium chloride, with the aid of the above diagram, and given the following data.

Lattice Breaking Enthalpy of strontium chloride	=	$+2128$ kJ mol^{-1}
Hydration Enthalpy of Sr^{2+}	=	-1484 kJ mol^{-1}
Hydration Enthalpy of Cl^{-}	=	-364 kJ mol^{-1}

13.   RADIOACTIVE HALF-LIFE

When a radioactive isotope emits radiation, the intensity of the radiation decreases with time, according to the graph shown below.

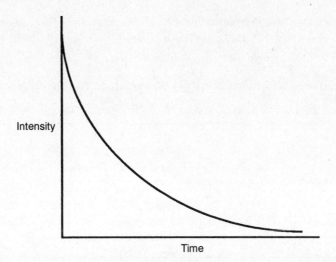

A feature of radioactive decay is that a quantity known as **half-life** (symbol $t_{1/2}$), which is a constant for any specified radioisotope, can be measured. This is the time during which the intensity of the radiation decreases to **half** what it was at the start of timing. Half-life values vary from fractions of a second to many millions of years; for example the half-life of ^{213}Po is $4{\cdot}2 \times 10^{-6}$ seconds, while that of ^{40}K is $1{\cdot}3 \times 10^{9}$ years.

A simple illustration of how half-life can be calculated is shown in the graph below.

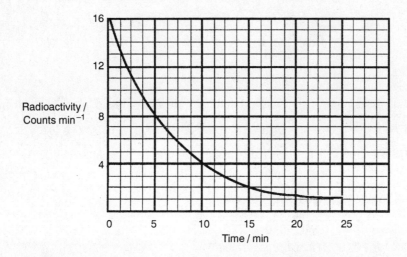

As can be seen, at the start of timing (time = 0), the radioactivity has a value of 16 counts min^{-1}. After 5 minutes, the count rate has dropped to 8 counts min^{-1}, i.e. to **half** the original value. After a further 5 minutes, the count rate has dropped from 8 to 4 counts min^{-1}, again a halving of the radioactivity. It can be seen from the graph that in any period of 5 minutes, the radioactivity decreases by half. The value of 5 minutes is thus the **half-life** for this particular radioisotope.

111

Half-life problems involve three quantities:

(a) **The half-life**. As mentioned before, this is a constant for the particular radioisotope and is entirely independent of how old the sample is, or whether the radioisotope is in the form of the pure element or in a compound.

(b) **The time over which the decay of the radioisotope has been measured**. This can be expressed in the usual units of time, e.g. 20 minutes, 500 years, etc. It can also be expressed as a number of half-lives, since the half-life for the radioisotope is an actual amount of time.

(c) **The quantity of the radioisotope or the intensity of the radiation**. This can be expressed in a number of ways:

* If the quantity of the radioisotope (or the intensity of the radiation) at the start of timing is referred to as 1 or 100% (i.e. the original or whole amount), we can refer to the sample having decayed to a fraction or a percentage of its original value, e.g. 1/2 (50%), 1/4 (25%) etc.

* The intensity of the radiation, as measured by a Geiger counter, is given in counts per minute. This is proportional to the quantity of the radioactive isotope present.

* The mass of the radiosotope present. Care is needed in using mass, since, although the **mass of the original radioisotope** is decreasing, the **total mass of the sample** may not change much or at all. For example, when radioactive, ^{209}Pb atoms decay, they do so by ß-emission and become atoms of ^{209}Bi. If we started with a 1 g sample of ^{209}Pb, we would eventually end up with a 1 g sample of ^{209}Bi, since ß-emission involves (virtually) no loss of mass. The mass of radioactive Pb would have been constantly decreasing, but the total mass of the sample would have remained the same. With α-emission, a small loss of total mass takes place. For example, ^{210}Po is an α-emitter, which turns into ^{206}Pb. A 210 g sample of ^{210}Po would decay eventually into 206 g of ^{206}Pb, the other 4 g having been lost as α-particles.

How to approach problems involving half-life can best be seen by considering the following Worked Examples.

WORKED EXAMPLE 13.1

A radioisotope has a half-life of 5 minutes. How long will it take for the radioactive count rate to drop to 12.5% of its original value?

Since we are given a **percentage** value of the original isotope, we describe the original quantity as being 100% (i.e. the whole amount). We proceed as follows.

> **At start** we have 100% of the original count rate
> **After 1 half-life** we have 50% of the original count rate
> **After 2 half-lives** we have 25% of the original count rate
> **After 3 half-lives** we have 12·5% of the original count rate.

So, in a period of time of 3 half-lives, the count rate has dropped to 12·5% of its original value. Since we are told that the half-life is 5 minutes, we conclude that the sample has been decaying for 3 × 5 = **15 minutes**.

WORKED EXAMPLE 13.2

A radioisotope has a half-life of 3 days. What fraction of the original isotope will be present if a pure sample of it decays for 12 days?

The sample has a half-life of 3 days and has been allowed to decay for 12 days; this is a time of **4 half-lives**.

Since we are asked for a **fraction** of the original isotope, we describe the original quantity as being 1 (i.e. the whole amount). We proceed as follows.

At start	we have 1 (the original amount)
After 1 half-life	we have 1/2 of the original amount
After 2 half-lives	we have 1/4 of the original amount
After 3 half-lives	we have 1/8 of the original amount
After 4 half-lives	we have 1/16 of the original amount.

So there will be 1/16th of the original radioisotope left after 4 half-lives.

WORKED EXAMPLE 13.3

A sample of a radioisotope has count rate, measured by a Geiger counter, of 48 counts per minute. 6 hours later, the count rate is 3 counts min^{-1} (counts per minute). What is the half-life of the radioisotope?

Since we are given the initial "amount" of the radioisotope in terms of its count rate, we proceed as follows.

At start	the count rate is 48 counts min^{-1}
After 1 half-life	the count rate is 24 counts min^{-1}
After 2 half-lives	the count rate is 12 counts min^{-1}
After 3 half-lives	the count rate is 6 counts min^{-1}
After 4 half-lives	the count rate is 3 counts min^{-1}

In a period of time of 4 half-lives, the count rate has dropped to 3 counts per minute. But we are told that this period of time is 6 hours.

So 1 half-life must be $\dfrac{6}{4}$ = **1·5 hours.**

PROBLEMS 13.1 to 13.20

The following problems are of the types shown in Worked Examples 13.1 to 13.3.

13. 1 A sample of a radioisotope decays to 1/8th of its original activity over a period of 12 days. What is the half-life of the radioisotope?

13. 2 A radioisotope has a half-life of 14 hours. How long will it take to decay to 6·25% of its original activity?

13. 3 A radioisotope with a half-life of 9 seconds has a count rate of 64 counts min^{-1} at the start of timing. What will the count rate be 18 seconds later?

13. 4 A sample of a radioisotope decays to 1/32 of its original activity in 12·5 years. What is the half-life of the isotope?

13. 5 Over what period of time would a radioisotope with a half-life of 8·3 days decay to 12·5% of its original activity?

13. 6 What fraction of its original activity will a sample of a radioisotope with a half-life of 3 minutes have after decaying for 15 minutes?

13. 7 A radioisotope decays to 1/16 of its original activity over a period of 20 minutes. What is its half-life?

13. 8 Over what period of time would a radioisotope, with a half-life of 7 seconds, decay in activity from 80 to 10 counts min^{-1}?

13. 9 A radioisotope has a half-life of 160 days. A 1 g sample of the pure radioisotope is allowed to decay for 640 days. What mass of the original isotope will remain after that time?

13.10 A radioisotope decays from an activity of 56 to 7 counts per minute over a period of 3·6 hours. What is the half-life of the radioisotope?

13.11 ^{257}Lr has a half-life of 8 seconds. Over what period of time would the activity of sample of this radioisotope decay from 120 to 15 counts min^{-1}?

13.12 ^{253}No has a half-life of 10 minutes. What percentage of this radioisotope would remain after a sample had decayed for a period of 20 minutes?

13.13 A sample of the radioisotope ^{24}Na decays to 1/32 of its original activity over a period of 75 hours. What is the half-life of ^{24}Na?

13.14 A sample of ^{254}Es, with a half-life of 280 days, has a count rate of 96 counts min^{-1}. How long will it take for the activity to decay to 12 counts per minute?

13.15 ^{90}Sr has a half-life of 27 years. What fraction of a sample of this radioisotope would remain after 108 years?

13.16 Tritium, ^{3}H, one of the heavy isotopes of hydrogen, decays to 1/64 of its original activity in 73·8 years. What is the half-life of this isotope?

13.17 ^{210}At has a half-life of 8·3 hours. Over what period of time would its activity decay to 1/64 of its original value?

13.18 ^{253}Fm has a half-life of 4·5 days. What percentage of a sample of this radioisotope would remain after decaying for 22·5 days?

13.19 ^{36}Cl decays to 6·25% of its original value in 1·2 × 10^{6} years. What is the half-life of this isotope?

13.20 ^{40}K has a half-life of 1·3 × 10^{9} years. After what period time would its activity decay to 6·25% of its original value?

Additional Theory: Dating Old Materials Using Carbon-14

A certain amount of radioactive carbon-14 is formed continuously in the upper atmosphere and is taken in by plants in the form of carbon dioxide during photosynthesis. Animals which eat these plants also absorb this radioactivity. It is thought that the level of radioactivity in the upper atmosphere has been constant for thousands of years, so we can assume that the level of radioactivity in a plant growing thousands of years ago is the same as that of a plant growing today. When a plant dies, or is eaten by an animal, it no longer absorbs carbon dioxide from the air and the amount of radioactivity in it decays. Since we know the half-life of carbon-14 (5570 years), we can use this fact to determine the age of animal and plant remains many thousands of years old. This is known as carbon dating. This is best illustrated by the following Worked Example.

WORKED EXAMPLE 13.4

An ancient animal skin coat is analysed for radioactivity from carbon-14; this level is found to be 12·5% of the level of radioactivity from a living plant. How old is the ancient animal skin coat?

We assume that the level of radioactivity from the animal skin coat, **at the time the animal was alive**, was the same as the level in animals and plants alive today. Since the level of radioactivity is expressed as a percentage of the original value, we proceed as follows.

When the animal was alive	the count rate would be 100% of that of living things today.
After 1 half-life	the count rate would be 50% of that of living things today.
After 2 half lives	the count rate would be 25% of that of living things today.
After 3 half-lives	the count rate would be 12·5% of that of living things today.

In a period of time of **3 half-lives**, the level of radioactivity in the animal skin coat would have decayed to 12·5% of that of current animal or plant material. But we know that the half-life of carbon-14 is 5570 years so we can say that the age of the coat is:

3 × 5570 = 16 710 years

PROBLEMS 13.21 to 13.25

The following problems involve the use of "carbon dating" illustrated in Worked Example 13.4.

In each of these problems take the half-life of carbon-14 to be 5570 years.

13.21 A sample of ancient wood is found to have a radioactive count rate due to carbon-14 of 12 counts min⁻¹. A sample of modern wood has a count rate of 48 counts min⁻¹. Calculate the age of the sample of ancient wood.

13.22 A leather garment is calculated to be 16 710 years old, using carbon dating. If a similar sample of modern leather has a carbon-14 count rate of 32 counts min⁻¹, what will the count rate from the ancient leather sample be?

13.23 A sample of ancient charred wood found in a Stone Age cave has a count rate of 1/32 of that of modern wood. Calculate the age of the charred wood.

13.24 A sample of bone found in a prehistoric dwelling has a carbon-14 count rate which is 12·5% of that of a similar sample of bone in a living person. Calculate the age of the prehistoric bone.

13.25 A fossilised tree sample has a count rate of 6 counts min⁻¹ due to carbon-14. A similar sample cut from a living tree has a count rate of 96 counts min⁻¹. Calculate the age of the fossil.

14. CALCULATIONS FROM EQUATIONS — 1

Calculations in which we are told the quantity of one of the chemical species in a reaction and asked to work out the quantity of another species can be solved by the use of the methods described below. The work of this chapter contains some work which is mainly a revision of Standard Grade at Credit Level; however, such problems should not be regarded as being trivial as many of them are of a type which could appear in the Higher examination. The method outlined may seem unnecessarily long, but only because **all** working and reasoning is shown. Although there **are** "short cuts", these do not actually involve a different **method**; they merely save time by omitting to show all the working. Such short cuts are not recommended until the method has been completely mastered.

WORKED EXAMPLE 14.1

What mass of copper would be obtained by heating 4 g of copper(II) oxide with an excess of carbon?

Step 1: Balanced Equation

$$2CuO + C \longrightarrow 2Cu + CO_2$$

Step 2: Mole Statement

The purpose of this is to connect the number of moles of what you are told about (the "known" species) with the number of moles of what you are asked about (the "unknown" species). This obtained directly from the balanced equation.

	2 mol of CuO	produce	2 mol of Cu
So	1 mol of CuO	produces	1 mol of Cu

Step 3: Calculation of "known moles"

In this step we calculate the number of moles of the "known" substance. In this example, we are told the **mass of copper(II) oxide**. So we calculate what 1 mol of copper(II) oxide weighs and work out from that how many moles 4 g represents.

$$1 \quad \text{mol of CuO} = 64 + 16 = 80 \text{ g}$$

$$80 \text{ g} \quad = \quad 1 \quad \text{mol of CuO}$$

$$1 \text{ g} \quad = \quad \frac{1}{80} \quad \text{mol of CuO}$$

$$4 \text{ g} \quad = \quad \frac{4}{80} \quad \text{mol of CuO}$$

$$= \quad \textbf{0·05 mol of CuO}$$

Step 4: Calculation of "unknown moles"

In this step we refer back to the mole statement (Step 2) and use the number of "known moles" that we have just calculated to obtain the number of "unknown moles":

1	mol of CuO	produces	1	mol of Cu
0·05	mol of CuO	produces	**0·05**	**mol of Cu**

Step 5: Finishing Off

In this last step, we convert the number of "unknown moles" that we have just worked out into the quantity that the question is asking about. In this example, we are asked to obtain the **mass of copper**.

1	mol of Cu	=	64 g
0·05	mol of Cu	=	0·05 × 64 g
		=	**3·2 g**

PROBLEMS 14.1 – 14.10

These problems are simple ones of the type illustrated by Worked Example 14.1.

14. 1 $Mg + H_2SO_4 \longrightarrow MgSO_4 + H_2$

What mass of hydrogen gas would be evolved if 6 g of magnesium reacted completely with dilute sulphuric acid?

14. 2 $CuO + H_2 \longrightarrow Cu + H_2O$

What mass of copper metal would be obtained by the complete reduction of 16 g of copper(II) oxide by hydrogen gas?

14. 3 $2PbO + C \longrightarrow 2Pb + CO_2$

What mass of carbon would be needed to reduce 22·3 g of lead(II) oxide completely to lead metal and carbon dioxide?

14. 4 $2CO + O_2 \longrightarrow 2CO_2$

What mass of carbon monoxide would require to be completely burned in oxygen to form 5·5 g of carbon dioxide?

14. 5 $2Na + 2H_2O \longrightarrow 2NaOH + H_2$

0·5 g of hydrogen gas is given off when sodium is reacted completely with water. What was the mass of sodium which reacted?

14. 6 $Zn + 2HCl \longrightarrow ZnCl_2 + H_2$

13 g of zinc is reacted with excess hydrochloric acid. What mass of hydrogen would be produced?

14. 7 $Mg + 2CH_3COOH \longrightarrow Mg(CH_3COO)_2 + H_2$

What mass of magnesium will completely react with 36 g of pure ethanoic acid, CH_3COOH?

14. 8 $Na_2CO_3 + H_2SO_4 \longrightarrow Na_2SO_4 + CO_2 + H_2O$

5·3 g of sodium carbonate is reacted with an excess of sulphuric acid. What mass of carbon dioxide would be evolved?

14. 9 $C_6H_{12}O_6 + 6O_2 \longrightarrow 6CO_2 + 6H_2O$

45 g of glucose is burned completely in an excess of oxygen. What mass of carbon dioxide would be produced?

14.10 $2Ag_2CO_3 \longrightarrow 4Ag + 2CO_2 + O_2$

What mass of oxygen would be produced by the complete thermal (by heat) decomposition of 22·08 g of silver(I) carbonate?

WORKED EXAMPLE 14.2

Hydrazine, N_2H_4, s a rocket fuel which reacts with oxygen producing gaseous products of nitrogen and water vapour under very high pressures. If 6.4×10^4 kg of hydrazine is burned completely, what mass of water vapour will be produced?

The difference between this and the previous question is that the mass(es) involved are expressed in more typical industrial quantities. The easiest way to approach this is to work out an answer as if the question had referred to 6·4 g of hydrazine; the conversion to kg can wait until the final step of the problem.

Step 1: Balanced Equation

$$N_2H_4 \ + \ O_2 \longrightarrow N_2 \ + \ 2H_2O$$

Step 2: Mole Statement

1 mol of N_2H_4 reacts to form 2 mol of H_2O

Step 3: "Known" Moles

"Known" substance is N_2H_4

$$32 \ \text{g of } N_2H_4 \ = \ 1 \ \text{mol}$$

$$1 \ \text{g of } N_2H_4 \ = \ \frac{1}{32} \ \text{mol}$$

$$6.4 \ \text{g of } N_2H_4 \ = \ \frac{6.4}{32} \ \text{mol}$$

$$= \ \textbf{0.2 mol of } N_2H_4$$

Step 4: "Unknown" Moles

"Unknown" is H_2O

From the Mole Statement:

1 mol of N_2H_4 reacts to form 2 mol of H_2O

So   0·2 mol of N_2H_4 reacts to form **0·4 mol of H_2O**

Step 5: Finishing Off

$$1 \ \text{mol of } H_2O \ = \ 18 \text{ g}$$

So $0.4 \ \text{mol of } H_2O \ = \ 0.4 \times 18 \text{ g}$

$$= \ \textbf{7.2 g}$$

This would be the end of the question if it has asked us about the reaction of 6·4 g of N_2H_4; however, the question referred to 6.4×10^4 kg of N_2H_4. A simple bit of direct proportion gives us the answer:

6·4 g   of N_2H_4 reacts to form 7·2 g   of H_2O

6.4×10^4 kg of N_2H_4 reacts to form 7.2×10^4 kg of H_2O

PROBLEMS 14.11 – 14.20

These problems of the type illustrated by Worked Example 14.2 involve masses in "industrial" quantities, often using "Standard Form", e.g. 3×10^3 kg, to express masses.

14.11 $$2SO_2 + O_2 \longrightarrow 2SO_3$$

Assuming 100% conversion of reactants to products, what mass of sulphur dioxide would be required to produce 160 kg of sulphur trioxide by the Contact Process described by the above equation?

14.12 $$N_2 + 3H_2 \longrightarrow 2NH_3$$

175 kg of nitrogen is completely converted to ammonia in the Haber Process represented by the above equation. What mass of hydrogen must have reacted?

14.13 $$Fe_2O_3 + 3C \longrightarrow 4Fe + 3CO_2$$

64 kg of iron(III) oxide is completely reduced by carbon to form pure iron. What mass of iron would be obtained?

14.14 $$2SO_2 + O_2 \longrightarrow 2SO_3$$

768 kg of sulphur dioxide is completely converted to sulphur trioxide by the above process. What mass of sulphur trioxide would be obtained?

14.15 $$C_2H_4 + H_2O \longrightarrow C_2H_5OH$$

Ethanol, C_2H_5OH, can be produced industrially by the catalytic reaction of ethene with steam. What mass of ethene would be needed to produce 1104 kg of ethanol?

14.16 $$3NO_2 + H_2O \longrightarrow 2HNO_3 + NO$$

The final stage in the industrial production of nitric acid, HNO_3, involves the above reaction. What mass of nitrogen dioxide must react to produce $2 \cdot 52 \times 10^3$ kg of nitric acid?

14.17 $$C_2H_2 + H_2O \longrightarrow CH_3CHO$$

The above equation shows the catalytic hydration of ethyne, C_2H_2, to ethanal, CH_3CHO. If $2 \cdot 08 \times 10^4$ kg of ethyne is completely reacted, what mass of ethanal would be produced?

14.18 $$TiCl_4 + 4Na \longrightarrow Ti + 4NaCl$$

Titanium metal can be extracted from titanium chloride by displacement by sodium. What mass of sodium would be needed to react completely with $7 \cdot 6 \times 10^3$ kg of titanium chloride?

14.19 $$N_2H_4 + 2F_2 \longrightarrow N_2 + 4HF$$

Hydrazine, N_2H_4, is used as a rocket fuel; it has been suggested that it would be very effective when mixed with fluorine as the above reaction gives out considerable energy. What mass of fluorine would be required to react completely with 8×10^4 kg of hydrazine?

14.20 $$CH_3CHO + 3Cl_2 \longrightarrow CCl_3CHO + 3HCl$$

What mass of ethanal, CH_3CHO, would react with an excess of chlorine to produce $2 \cdot 95 \times 10^4$ kg of trichloroethanal, CCl_3CHO?

WORKED EXAMPLE 14.3

Ethene reacts with chlorine to form dichloroethane, a starting material in the formation of the plastic formerly known as PVC. 1.75×10^4 kg of ethene is introduced into the reaction chamber with an excess of chlorine, but only 80% of it reacts in the given time. What mass of dichloroethane will have been produced?

In many industrial processes, reactions do not go "to completion", with 100% of the reactants being used up to give 100% "yield". In any given period of time, only a certain percentage of the materials will react to give the required product, with unreacted materials being recycled through the plant. The method used to solve the problem is only slightly different from that described in the last example.

Step 1: Balanced Equation

$$C_2H_4 + Cl_2 \longrightarrow C_2H_4Cl_2$$

Step 2: Mole Statement

$$\text{1 mol of } C_2H_4 \text{ reacts to form 1 mol of } C_2H_4Cl_2$$

Step 3: "Known" Moles

As in the previous example, we will deal with the amount of the "known" C_2H_4 in units of grams and convert to the required unit of kg at the end of the problem. So we will regard our mass of $C_2H_4 = 1.75$ g. But we are told that only 80% of this reacts, so our mass of "known" C_2H_4 is actually:

$$80\% \text{ of } 1.75 \text{ g} = 0.8 \times 1.75 = 1.4 \text{ g}$$

Having obtained the actual amount of C_2H_4 reacting, we proceed as before.

$$28 \text{ g of } C_2H_4 = 1 \text{ mol of } C_2H_4$$

$$1 \text{ g of } C_2H_4 = \frac{1}{28} \text{ mol of } C_2H_4$$

$$1.4 \text{ g of } C_2H_4 = \frac{1.4}{28} \text{ mol of } C_2H_4$$

$$= \textbf{0.05 mol of } C_2H_4$$

Step 4: Calculation of "Unknown" Moles

From the Mole Statement:

$$1 \text{ mol of } C_2H_4 \text{ reacts to give 1 mol of } C_2H_4Cl_2$$

So $\quad$ 0.05 mol of C_2H_4 reacts to form 0.05 mol of $C_2H_4Cl_2$

Step 5: Finishing Off

$$1 \text{ mol of } C_2H_4Cl_2 = 99 \text{ g}$$

So $\quad$ 0.05 mol of $C_2H_4Cl_2 = 0.05 \times 99$ g

$$= \textbf{4.95 g}$$

As in the previous Worked Example, we convert this to the quantities *actually* involved:

$\quad$ 1.75 g $\quad$ of C_2H_4 (80% reacting) produced 4.95 g $\quad$ of $C_2H_4Cl_2$

So $\quad$ 1.75×10^4 kg of C_2H_4 (80% reacting) produces 4.95×10^4 kg of $C_2H_4Cl_2$

PROBLEMS 14.21 – 14.30

These problems of the type illustrated by Worked Example 14.3 involve using percentage yields to calculate masses of reactant or product.

14.21
$$Fe_2O_3 + 3CO \longrightarrow 2Fe + 3CO_2$$

Iron (III) oxide can be reduced to iron by carbon monoxide. 2×10^3 kg of iron(III) oxide is treated with carbon monoxide, but only 80% by mass reacts. What mass of carbon monoxide will have been used in the process?

14.22
$$CaCO_3 \longrightarrow CaO + CO_2$$

Calcium carbonate can be decomposed to calcium oxide by heat. A form of rock which is 60% calcium carbonate by mass is crushed and heated until all the calcium carbonate has decomposed. If 4×10^3 kg of rock is so treated, what mass of calcium oxide could theoretically be obtained?

14.23
$$CH_4 + H_2O \longrightarrow 3H_2 + CO$$

Methane can be reacted with steam to form hydrogen and carbon monoxide although, under the reaction conditions, only 30% methane, by mass, reacts. Under these conditions, if 4×10^4 kg of methane is introduced to the reaction chamber, what mass of hydrogen would be produced?

14.24
$$2PbS + 3O_2 \longrightarrow 2PbO + 2SO_2$$

The mineral galena, lead(II) sulphide, can be converted to lead(II) oxide by reaction with oxygen. If 47·8 kg of galena is so treated, but there is only a 65% yield, what mass of lead(II) oxide would be produced?

14.25
$$TiCl_4 + 2Mg \longrightarrow Ti + 2MgCl_2$$

In the conversion of titanium(IV) chloride to titanium, using an excess of magnesium, a 60% yield of product is obtained under certain conditions. If $1·14 \times 10^4$ kg of titanium(IV) chloride is so treated, what mass of titanium would be obtained?

14.26
$$N_2 + 3H_2 \longrightarrow 2NH_3$$

In the manufacture of ammonia by the Haber Process, under certain conditions, there is only a 70% yield of product. If $8·40 \times 10^4$ kg of nitrogen is reacted with an excess of hydrogen under these conditions, calculate the mass of ammonia produced.

14.27
$$C_6H_{12}O_6 \longrightarrow 2C_2H_5OH + 2CO_2$$

The fermentation of glucose to ethanol and carbon dioxide produces a 75% yield of ethanol under certain conditions. If 72 kg of glucose is fermented under these conditions, what mass of ethanol would be produced?

14.28
$$2SO_2 + O_2 \longrightarrow 2SO_3$$

In the manufacture of sulphur trioxide from sulphur dioxide, as a preliminary stage in the manufacture of sulphuric acid, $7·68 \times 10^4$ kg of sulphur dioxide is introduced to the reaction chamber in the presence of an excess of oxygen over a period of time. If the reaction goes to 60% completion, calculate the mass of sulphur trioxide produced in this time.

14.29
$$2ZnS + 3O_2 \longrightarrow 2ZnO + 2SO_2$$

Zinc sulphide can be converted by the above reaction to form zinc oxide, from which zinc metal can then be extracted. If $1 \cdot 94 \times 10^4$ kg of ore which is known to contain 40% zinc oxide by mass is so treated, what mass of zinc oxide would be obtained? (Assume that all the available zinc sulphide reacts according to the above equation.)

14.30
$$CH_3COOH + CH_3OH \longrightarrow CH_3COOCH_3 + H_2O$$

In the above esterification of ethanoic acid with methanol to form methyl ethanoate and water, 7·5 g of ethanoic acid, CH_3COOH, is heated with an excess of methanol in the presence of a sulphuric acid catalyst. If there is a 72% yield of product, calculate the mass of methyl ethanoate which this represents.

WORKED EXAMPLE 14.4

Ammonia can be oxidised in the presence of oxygen and a catalyst to nitrogen monoxide. In a certain period of time, $1 \cdot 36 \times 10^3$ kg of ammonia enters the reaction chamber and $1 \cdot 68 \times 10^3$ kg of nitrogen monoxide is produced. Calculate the percentage yield of the nitrogen monoxide in this process.

In this type of problem, we calculate the mass of product that would have been expected if the reaction had gone to completion. Then, in the final stage, we express the mass actually obtained as a percentage of the theoretical mass.

Step 1: Balanced Equation

$$4NH_3 + 5O_2 \longrightarrow 4NO + 6H_2O$$

Step 2: Mole Statement

Assuming for the moment that the reaction goes to completion,

4 mol of NH_3 produces 4 mol of NO

1 mol of NH_3 produces 1 mol of NO

Step 3: Calculation of "Known" Moles

As with previous problems involving the use of "Standard Form" (or "Scientific Notation") and units such as kg, we will ignore, for the time being, the 10^3 kg part and work it out as though the problem had referred to 1·36 g ammonia.

$$17 \ \text{g} = 1 \ \text{mol of } NH_3$$

$$1 \ \text{g} = \frac{1}{17} \ \text{mol of } NH_3$$

$$1 \cdot 36 \ \text{g} = \frac{1 \cdot 36}{17} \ \text{mol of } NH_3$$

$$= \textbf{0·08 mol of } NH_3$$

Step 4: "Unknown" Moles

Assuming the reaction goes to completion,

1 mol of NH_3 produces 1 mol of NO

0·08 mol of NH_3 produces 0·08 mol of NO

Step 5: Finishing Off

1 mol of NO weighs 30 g

0·08 mol of NO weighs 0·08 × 30 g

= **2·4 g**

This is the mass of NO which would have obtained from the complete reaction of 1·36 g of NH_3. The problem, however, referred to $1·36 \times 10^3$ kg of NH_3.

1·36 g of NH_3 would produce 2·4 g of NO
(if completely reacted)

$1·36 \times 10^3$ kg of NH_3 would produce $2·4 \times 10^3$ kg of NO
(if completely reacted)

In the problem we are told that $1·68 \times 10^3$ kg of NO are produced; we are asked to express this as a percentage yield, that is a percentage of the amount that would be produced if the reaction had gone to completion.

$$\% \text{ yield } = \frac{\text{actual mass obtained}}{\text{maximum possible mass}} \times 100$$

$$= \frac{1·68 \times 10^3}{2·4 \times 10^3} \times 100$$

$$= \mathbf{70\%}$$

PROBLEMS 14.31 – 14.40

These problems are of a type similar to Worked Example 14.4, in which percentage yield of a product or percentage purity of a reactant require to be calculated.

14.31

$$CO + 2H_2 \longrightarrow CH_3OH$$

Carbon monoxide and hydrogen gas can be reacted in the presence of a catalyst to form methanol, CH_3OH. Under particular reaction conditions, 224 kg of carbon monoxide is mixed with an excess of hydrogen in the catalyst chamber during the course of a day. Methanol is continuously removed and unreacted gases recycled. After this time, 192 kg of methanol has been produced.

(a) Calculate the mass of methanol which would have been formed *had all the carbon monoxide reacted*.

(b) Express the mass of methanol *actually produced* as a percentage (the "percentage yield") of the theoretical mass calculated at part *(a)*.

14.32

$$C_2H_4 + HI \longrightarrow C_2H_5I$$

Ethene reacts with hydrogen iodide to form iodoethane, C_2H_5I. Under certain conditions, $3·5 \times 10^4$ kg of ethene enters the reaction chamber every 24 hours, with $7·8 \times 10^4$ kg of iodoethane being produced in that time. Calculate the percentage yield of product, by mass, for this process.

14.33
$$2FeCL_2 + Cl_2 \longrightarrow 2FeCl_3$$

In reaction represented by the above equation, $5 \cdot 08 \times 10^3$ kg of iron(II) chloride yields $3 \cdot 9 \times 10^3$ kg of iron(III) chloride under certain conditions. Calculate the percentage yield of product.

14.34
$$C_6H_6 + HNO_3 \longrightarrow C_6H_5NO_2 + H_2O$$

$187 \cdot 2$ kg of benzene, C_6H_6, enters a reaction chamber with an excess of nitric acid. After a time, $221 \cdot 2$ kg of nitrobenzene, $C_6H_5NO_2$, is obtained. Calculate the percentage yield of product.

14.35
$$2Cu_2S + 3O_2 \longrightarrow 2Cu_2O + 2SO_2$$

$1 \cdot 4 \times 10^5$ kg of copper(I) sulphide is heated with an excess of oxygen, producing $7 \cdot 56 \times 10^4$ kg of copper(I) oxide. Express this latter mass as a percentage yield of product.

14.36
$$CH_3COOH + C_2H_5OH \longrightarrow CH_3COOC_2H_5 + H_2O$$

$14 \cdot 6$ g of ethanoic acid, CH_3COOH, is refluxed with an excess of ethanol in the presence of concentrated sulphuric acid (acting as a catalyst). This results in the production of $13 \cdot 92$ g of the ester, ethyl ethanoate; express this mass as a percentage yield.

14.37
$$Na_2CO_3 + H_2SO_4 \longrightarrow Na_2SO_4 + CO_2 + H_2O$$

A $5 \cdot 3$ g sample of impure sodium carbonate is reacted with an excess of sulphuric acid, resulting in $1 \cdot 76$ g of carbon dioxide being given off.

(a) Calculate the mass of pure sodium carbonate which must have been present in the sample.

(b) Express this as a percentage of the mass of the original, impure, sample. This is the "percentage purity" of original sample. (Assume that the impurity does not react with the acid to give off carbon dioxide.)

14.38
$$2SO_2 + O_2 \longrightarrow 2SO_3$$

The above equation represents the conversion of sulphur dioxide to sulphur trioxide. Over a period of time, $1 \cdot 6 \times 10^3$ kg of sulphur dioxide is introduced to the reaction chamber in the presence of an excess of oxygen. $1 \cdot 724 \times 10^3$ kg of sulphur trioxide is obtained during the process; express the mass of product as a percentage yield.

14.39
$$Fe + 2HCl \longrightarrow FeCl_2 + H_2$$

A $6 \cdot 3$ g nail, consisting mainly of iron, is reacted with an excess of dilute hydrochloric acid causing all the iron present to be converted to iron(II) chloride solution. After evaporation of the solution and the removal of all other substances, $11 \cdot 43$ g of pure, solid, iron(II) chloride is obtained.

(a) Calculate the mass of pure iron in the nail.

(b) Express the mass of iron calculated at *(a)* as a percentage of the mass of the nail.

14.40
$$Fe_2O_3 + 3CO \longrightarrow 2Fe + 3CO_2$$
$3 \cdot 125 \times 10^4$ kg of an iron ore which is impure iron(III) oxide is reacted with an excess of carbon monoxide, producing $1 \cdot 4 \times 10^4$ kg of iron. Calculate the percentage, by mass, of iron in the impure ore. (Assume that all the iron(III) oxide present is reduced to iron.)

15.   CALCULATIONS FROM EQUATIONS — 2

This chapter uses the same method as that of Chapter 14 to carry out calculations that involve the concentrations and volumes of solutions. It should be noted that the unit used for concentration (or molarity) in this book is mol l^{-1} ("moles per litre"). This unit is identical to the mol/l used at Standard Grade and the M ("Molar") of many text books. Calculations involving reactants in excess and those involving "redox" titrations are included here.

WORKED EXAMPLE 15.1

What volume of 0·5 mol l^{-1} sodium hydroxide solution will exactly neutralise 40 cm^3 of 0·2 mol l^{-1} sulphuric acid?

Step 1: Balanced Equation

$$2NaOH \; + \; H_2SO_4 \longrightarrow Na_2SO_4 \; + \; 2H_2O$$

Step 2: Mole Statement

2 mol of NaOH neutralise 1 mol of H_2SO_4

Step 3: Calculation of "Known" Moles

In this case we are told the **volume** and **concentration** of the sulphuric acid. This enables us to calculate the number of moles.

number of moles = volume (in litres) × concentration

= 0·04 × 0·2

= **0·008 mol (of H_2SO_4)**

Step 4: "Unknown" Moles

2 mol of NaOH neutralise 1 mol of H_2SO_4 (from Step 2)

Rewriting to put our "unknown", NaOH, on the right:

1 mol of H_2SO_4 is neutralised by 2 mol of NaOH

0·008 mol of H_2SO_4 is neutralised by 2 × 0·008 mol of NaOH

= **0·016 mol of NaOH**

Step 5: Finishing Off

The problem asks for the **volume** of NaOH solution. We are told in the problem that its concentration is 0·5 mol l^{-1} and we have just calculated that we need 0·016 mol of it. So we select the correct equation:

volume (in litres) = $\dfrac{\text{number of moles}}{\text{concentration}}$

= $\dfrac{0 \cdot 016}{0 \cdot 5}$

= **0·031 l (32 cm^3)**

PROBLEMS 15.1 – 15.15

These problems are of the type illustrated by Worked Example 15.1, involving concentrations of solutions, although the last 5 involve reagents which may be unfamiliar, but where enough information is given to write a Mole Statement and, hence, solve each problem using the same method as before.

15. 1
$$2KOH + H_2SO_4 \longrightarrow K_2SO_4 + 2H_2O$$

50 cm^3 of 0·4 mol l^{-1} potassium hydroxide solution exactly neutralises 20 cm^3 of sulphuric acid. What concentration was the acid?

15. 2
$$2NaOH + H_2SO_4 \longrightarrow Na_2SO_4 + 2H_2O$$

20 cm^3 of 0·2 mol l^{-1} sulphuric acid exactly neutralises a quantity of 0·5 mol l^{-1} sodium hydroxide solution. What volume of the alkali must have been reacted?

15. 3
$$2KOH + CO_2 \longrightarrow K_2CO_3 + H_2O$$

50 cm^3 of 0·5 mol l^{-1} potassium hydroxide solution is reacted with an excess of carbon dioxide. What mass of potassium carbonate would be obtained upon complete evaporation of the water from the resulting solution?

15. 4
$$H_3PO_4 + 3NaOH \longrightarrow Na_3PO_4 + 3H_2O$$

1·96 g of pure phosphoric acid, H_3PO_4, is dissolved in water and the solution is exactly neutralised by a quantity of 0·2 mol l^{-1} sodium hydroxide solution. What volume of the alkali solution must have been required?

15. 5
$$2NH_3 + H_2SO_4 \longrightarrow (NH_4)_2SO_4$$

6·8 g of ammonia gas is required to neutralise exactly 250 cm^3 of sulphuric acid. What concentration must the acid have been?

15. 6
$$C_6H_4(COOH)_2 + 2NaOH \longrightarrow C_6H_4(COONa)_2 + 2H_2O$$

A solution of phthalic acid, $C_6H_4(COOH)_2$, is exactly neutralised by 25 cm^3 of a 2 mol l^{-1} solution of sodium hydroxide. What mass of phthalic acid must have been dissolved in the original solution?

15. 7
$$CH_3COOH + NaOH \longrightarrow CH_3COONa + H_2O$$

A 20 cm^3 sample of vinegar (dilute ethanoic acid, CH_3COOH) is titrated with standard 0·1 mol l^{-1} sodium hydroxide solution. Exactly 36·4 cm^3 of the alkali is found to neutralise the acid sample. What is the concentration, in mol l^{-1}, of the acid in the vinegar sample?

15. 8
$$H_2SO_4 + BaCl_2 \longrightarrow BaSO_4 + 2HCl$$

12·5 cm^3 of a 0·4 mol l^{-1} solution of sulphuric acid is poured into a solution containing an excess of barium chloride. A precipitate of barium sulphate is formed which is filtered, washed, dried and weighed. What mass of precipitate should theoretically be obtained?

15. 9
$$2KOH + (COOH)_2 \longrightarrow (COOK)_2 + 2H_2O$$

A solution of oxalic acid, $(COOH)_2$, is standardised by taking a 25 cm^3 sample of it and titrating it against 0·2 mol l^{-1} potassium hydroxide solution. Neutralisation is obtained by the addition of 23·5 cm^3 of the alkali. Calculate the concentration, in mol l^{-1}, of the acid.

15.10
$$Pb(NO_3)_2 + H_2SO_4 \longrightarrow PbSO_4 + 2HNO_3$$

20 cm^3 of dilute sulphuric acid is reacted with an excess of lead(II) nitrate, causing 1·212 g of lead(II) sulphate to be precipitated. Calculate the concentration, in mol l^{-1}, of the acid.

15.11 A compound known as ethylenediaminetetraacetic acid (EDTA) is useful for measuring the quantities of certain metal ions in solution. For example, Ca^{2+} ions and EDTA react in a 1 mol : 1 mol ratio. It is found that 14·6 cm^3 of 0·1 mol l^{-1} EDTA solution reacts exactly with a 25 cm^3 sample of a solution containing Ca^{2+} ions. Calculate the concentration, in mol l^{-1}, of the calcium ion solution.

15.12 Potassium permanganate, in the presence of acid, reacts with sulphite ions in the ratio 1 mol permanganate : 2·5 mol sulphite. When all the permanganate has reacted, its purple colour disappears and the solution becomes clear. Thus, standard acidified potassium permanganate solution can be easily used to measure the concentration of sulphite ions in a solution.

17 cm^3 of standard 0·1 mol l^{-1} acidified potassium permanganate solution reacts exactly with 21·25 cm^3 of a solution containing sulphite ions. Calculate the concentration, in mol l^{-1}, of the sulphite ion solution.

15.13 Potassium dichromate, in the presence of acid, reacts with Fe^{2+} ions in the ratio 1 mol potassium dichromate : 6 mol Fe^{2+}. 25 cm^3 of a solution containing Fe^{2+} ions was titrated with 0·1 mol l^{-1} acidified potassium dichromate solution. It was found that 15 cm^3 of the dichromate solution exactly reacted with all the Fe^{2+} ions. Calculate the concentration, in mol l^{-1} of the Fe^{2+} solution.

15.14 EDTA solution reacts in a 1 mol : 1 mol ratio with Ni^{2+} ions under certain conditions. A 20 cm^3 sample of a nickel(II) solution was titrated with 0·05 mol l^{-1} EDTA solution; 48 cm^3 of the EDTA was required to react exactly with the Ni^{2+} ions. What concentration, in mol l^{-1}, is the nickel(II) solution?

15.15 Standard acidified potassium permanganate can be used to determine the concentration of hydrogen peroxide solution; the solutions react in the ratio 1 mol of potassium permanganate : 2·5 mol of hydrogen peroxide. In an analysis it is found that 16·8 cm^3 of standard 0·025 mol l^{-1} potassium permanganate solution reacts exactly with a 50 cm^3 sample of hydrogen peroxide solution. What is the concentration, in mol l^{-1}, of the hydrogen peroxide solution?

WORKED EXAMPLE 15.2

A sample of sulphuric acid is to be analysed by titration with sodium carbonate solution. A 25 cm^3 sample of it is pipetted into a 250 cm^3 standard flask and the solution is made up to the mark. A 25 cm^3 sample of this diluted solution is titrated with standard 0·2 mol l^{-1} sodium carbonate solution; it is found that 15 cm^3 of the sodium carbonate solution is required to neutralise the acid sample. What concentration was the *original (undiluted)* acid.

In problems which involve samples being diluted it is difficult to generalise about the best method. However, usually, dilutions are made in multiples of 10; when this is the case the problem can usually be solved without too much difficulty. In this problem, a 25 cm^3 sample is diluted to 250 cm^3; in other words *it has been diluted to 1/10th of its original concentration*. With that in mind, we can firstly work out the concentration of the *diluted* acid, and simply multiply this value by 10 to get the original concentration.

Step 1: Balanced Equation

$$Na_2CO_3 \; + \; H_2SO_4 \longrightarrow Na_2SO_4 \; + \; CO_2 \; + \; H_2O$$

Step 2: Mole Statement

1 mol of Na_2CO_3 neutralises 1 mol of H_2SO_4

Step 3: "Known" Moles

In this case we are told the **volume** and **concentration** of the sodium carbonate solution. This enables us to calculate the number of moles.

number of moles	=	number of litres	×	concentration
	=	0·015	×	0·02
	=	**0·003 mol (of Na$_2$CO$_3$)**		

Step 4: "Unknown" Moles

1   mol of Na_2CO_3 is neutralised by 1   mol of H_2SO_4

0·003 mol of Na_2CO_3 is neutralised by **0·003 mol of H$_2$SO$_4$**

Step 5: Finishing Off

We have to find the concentration of the (diluted) H_2SO_4 first, so we select the correct equation:

$$\text{concentration} \; = \; \frac{\text{number of moles}}{\text{number of litres}}$$

$$= \; \frac{0·003}{0·025}$$

$$= \; \textbf{0·12 mol } \textit{l}^{-1}$$

This is the concentration of the *diluted* acid. Since this acid solution was made by diluting the original acid to 1/10th of its concentration, the original acid has 10 times the concentration of the diluted sample. The original acid therefore has a concentration of $10 \times 0·12$ mol l^{-1}, that is **1·2 mol l^{-1}**.

PROBLEMS 15.16 – 15.20

These problems involve the dilution of solutions as in Worked Example 15.2

15.16 $2NaOH + H_2SO_4 \longrightarrow Na_2SO_4 + 2H_2O$

A 25 cm^3 sample of sulphuric acid of unknown concentration is pipetted into a 250 cm^3 standard flask and made up to the mark with water. A 25 cm^3 sample of the new, *diluted*, solution is titrated with 0·2 mol l^{-1} sodium hydroxide solution. 50 cm^3 of the alkali exactly neutralises this sample. Calculate:

(a)   the concentration of the *diluted* acid, in mol l^{-1};

(b)   how many times more concentrated the original sample is in comparison to the diluted sample;

(c)   the concentration of the *original acid* (using your answers to *(a)* and *(b)* above).

5.17 $CH_3COOH + KOH \longrightarrow CH_3COOK + H_2O$

30 g of pure ethanoic acid, CH_3COOH, is diluted with water to make up a 250 cm^3 standard solution. A 10 cm^3 sample of this diluted acid is withdrawn and titrated with 0·2 mol l^{-1} potassium hydroxide solution. Calculate:

(a)   the concentration, in mol l^{-1}, of the *diluted* acid;

(b)   the volume of alkali required to neutralise the 10 cm^3 sample.

15.18 $H_2SO_4 + Na_2CO_3 \longrightarrow Na_2SO_4 + CO_2 + H_2O$

12·25 g of pure sulphuric acid was weighed and made up to 1 l with water in a standard flask. A 40 cm^3 sample of this diluted solution was found to be neutralised exactly by 25 cm^3 of sodium carbonate solution. Calculate:

(a)   the concentration, in mol l^{-1}, of the diluted acid;

(b)   the concentration of the sodium carbonate solution.

15.19 $2NaOH + H_2SO_4 \longrightarrow Na_2SO_4 + 2H_2O$

Car batteries contain sulphuric acid. A 10 cm^3 sample of battery acid is pipetted into a 1 l standard flask and made up to the mark with water. A 50 cm^3 sample of the new diluted acid is titrated against standard 0·2 mol l^{-1} sodium hydroxide solution. It is found that 12·5 cm^3 of the alkali exactly neutralises the diluted acid sample. Calculate:

(a)   how *many times* more concentrated is the battery acid compared to the diluted acid;

(b)   the concentration of the diluted acid.

(c)   Use your answers to *(a)* and *(b)* to calculate the concentration of the battery acid, in mol l^{-1}.

15.20 $2HCl + Na_2CO_3 \longrightarrow 2NaCl + CO_2 + H_2O$

A standard 1 mol l^{-1} solution of sodium carbonate is made up. A 20 cm^3 sample is then withdrawn from it and pipetted into a 500 cm^3 standard flask which is made up to the mark with water. A 20 cm^3 sample of this *diluted solution* is titrated against hydrochloric acid of unknown concentration. 40 cm^3 of acid exactly neutralises the sample. Calculate:

(a)   how many moles of sodium carbonate are present in the first 20 cm^3 sample.

(b)   What is the concentration of the diluted sodium carbonate solution?

(c)   What is the concentration of the hydrochloric acid?

WORKED EXAMPLE 15.3

1·3 g of zinc is added to 25 cm³ of 2 mol l^{-1} hydrochloric acid. What mass of hydrogen gas will have been given off when the reaction is complete?

At first sight this problem seems no different from those considered earlier; however, closer examination reveals that we are told enough information to work out the number of moles of **both reactants**, the zinc **and** the hydrochloric acid. In a situation like this, almost invariably one of the reactants is in excess; that is, there is more of it than is able to react. We proceed as follows.

Step 1: Balanced Equation

$$Zn \ + \ 2HCl \ \longrightarrow \ ZnCl_2 \ + \ H_2$$

Step 2: Mole Statement

Since we are told the quantities of zinc and hydrochloric acid, and asked about hydrogen, we include all three in the statement:

1 mol of Zn reacts with 2 mol of HCl to produce 1 mol of H_2

Step 3: Calculation of "Known" Moles

Our problem here is that there are **two** reactants that are "known". We therefore need firstly to calculate the number of moles of each present.

$$Zn: \quad 65 \text{ g} \quad = \quad 1 \quad mol$$

$$1 \text{ g} \quad = \quad \frac{1}{65} \text{ mol}$$

$$1 \cdot 3 \text{ g} \quad = \quad \frac{1 \cdot 3}{65} \text{ mol}$$

$$= \quad \textbf{0·02 mol of Zn}$$

$$HCl: \quad \text{no. of moles} \quad = \quad \text{concentration} \ \times \ \text{no. of litres}$$

$$= \quad 2 \quad \times \quad 0 \cdot 025$$

$$= \quad \textbf{0·05 mol of HCl}$$

So we have 0·02 mol of Zn and 0·05 mol of HCl. But from the Mole Statement, we see that:

1 mol of Zn will react with 2 mol of HCl.

So   0·02 mol of Zn will react with 0·04 mol of HCl.

This means that we have too much (an excess of) HCl. Of the 0·05 mol that we have, only 0·04 mol will react, since that is the quantity which will use up all the zinc. So our "known" moles is either 0·02 mol of Zn or 0·04 mol of HCl. (It does not matter which we use, as should become apparent in the next step.)

Step 4: Calculation of "Unknown" Moles

1 mol of Zn reacts with 2 mol of HCl to produce 1 mol of H_2

0·02 mol of Zn reacts with 0·04 mol of HCl to produce **0·02 mol of H_2**

Step 5: Finishing Off

We have calculated that 0·02 mol of H_2 will be produced and we have to express this as a mass:

1 mol of H_2 =   2 g

0·02 mol of H_2 =   0·02 × 2 g

=   **0·04 g**

PROBLEMS 15.21 – 15.30

These problems are of the type illustrated in Worked Example 15.3, in which one of the reactants is in excess.

15.21 $Pb + 2HCl \longrightarrow PbCl_2 + H_2$

6·21 g of lead is added to 50 cm^3 of 1 mol l^{-1} hydrochloric acid. What mass of hydrogen gas will have been given off on completion of the reaction?

15.22 $CaCO_3 + 2HNO_3 \longrightarrow Ca(NO_3)_2 + CO_2 + H_2O$

12 g of calcium carbonate is placed in 500 cm^3 of 0·4 mol l^{-1} nitric acid. What mass of carbon dioxide would have been given off when the reaction was complete?

15.23 $Pb(NO_3)_2 + 2KI \longrightarrow PbI_2 + 2KNO_3$

120 cm^3 of 0·2 mol l^{-1} lead(II) nitrate solution is added to 200 cm^3 of 0·25 mol l^{-1} potassium iodide solution. The lead(II) iodide precipitate formed is filtered and dried. What is the theoretical mass of precipitate obtained?

15.24 $2CH_3COOH + Na_2CO_3 \longrightarrow 2CH_3COONa + CO_2 + H_2O$

3 g of pure ethanoic acid, CH_3COOH, is added to 90 cm^3 of 0·4 mol l^{-1} sodium carbonate solution. What mass of carbon dioxide will be evolved?

15.25 $CuO + H_2SO_4 \longrightarrow CuSO_4 + H_2O$

1·6 g of copper(II) oxide is added to a beaker of 50 cm^3 of 0·25 mol l^{-1} sulphuric acid. The mixture is heated and stirred until no further reaction takes place, and the contents of the beaker are filtered.

(a)   What mass of unreacted copper(II) oxide would be removed from the beaker by the filtration, after being dried?

(b)   The remaining solution is evaporated and dried to form anhydrous copper(II) sulphate, $CuSO_4$. What mass of copper(II) sulphate would be obtained?

15.26 $2AgNO_3 + MgCl_2 \longrightarrow 2AgCl + MgNO_3$

40 cm^3 of 0·045 mol l^{-1} silver(I) nitrate solution is added to 12 cm^3 of 0·1 mol l^{-1} magnesium chloride solution. What mass of silver(I) chloride would be precipitated?

15.27 $H_2SO_4 + BaCl_2 \longrightarrow BaSO_4 + 2HCl$

20 cm^3 of 0·2 mol l^{-1} sulphuric acid is added to 50 cm^3 of 0·1 mol l^{-1} barium chloride solution. What mass of barium sulphate would be precipitated?

15.28 $(NH_4)_2SO_4 + 2NaOH \longrightarrow Na_2SO_4 + 2H_2O + 2NH_3$

3·3 g of ammonium sulphate is added to 120 cm^3 of 0·5 mol l^{-1} sodium hydroxide solution and the solution heated. What is the theoretical mass of ammonia which would be evolved?

15.29 $FeS + 2HCl \longrightarrow FeCl_2 + H_2S$

4·4 g of iron(II) sulphate is added to 160 cm^3 of 0·5 mol l^{-1} hydrochloric acid. What is the maximum mass of hydrogen sulphide gas, H_2S, which will be given off?

15.30 $Al(NO_3)_3 + 3NaOH \longrightarrow Al(OH)_3 + 3NaNO_3$

40 cm^3 of 0·5 mol l^{-1} aluminium nitrate solution is added to 200 cm^3 of 0·4 mol l^{-1} sodium hydroxide solution. What mass of aluminium hydroxide would be precipitated?

WORKED EXAMPLE 15.4

The ion-electron equations below represent the oxidation and reduction reactions taking place when permanganate ions, MnO_4^-, in acid solution, reacts with iodide ions.

RED: $MnO_4^- + 8H^+ + 5e^- \longrightarrow Mn^{2+} + 4H_2O$

OX: $2I^- \longrightarrow I_2 + 2e^-$

20 cm^3 of a 0·2 mol l^{-1} solution of iodide ions is titrated with a 0·064 mol l^{-1} solution of permanganate ions, in acid solution. What volume of the permanganate solution will be required to react exactly with all the iodide ions?

This problem is actually not different from those done previously, except that the balanced equation for the reaction has not been given. Using the ion-electron equations given, it can be seen that the reduction reaction ("RED") involves the gain of 5 electrons, while the oxidation reaction ("OX") involves the loss of 2 electrons. Since the number of electrons being gained must be the same as that being lost, the balanced equation is obtained by multiplying the above equations as below:

2 × RED: $2 \times (MnO_4^- + 8H^+ + 5e^- \longrightarrow Mn^{2+} + 4H_2O)$

5 × OX: $5 \times (2I^- \longrightarrow I_2 + 2e^-)$

If the reduction is multiplied throughout by 2, we now have a **gain of 10 electrons**. The multiplication of the oxidation by 5 gives a **loss of 10 electrons**. That is, the two "half-reactions" are now balanced. The full balanced equation can be obtained by multiplying out the reduction and oxidation reactions, adding them together and cancelling out species common to each side. However, for the purpose of this problem, that is not necessary. What is important to see is that the combined reduction and oxidation reactions tell us that:

2 mol of MnO_4^- reacts with 10 mol of I^-

Or, more simply, 1 mol of MnO_4^- reacts with 5 mol of I^-

Thus, we have established "Step 2: Mole Statement", in which the number of moles of the species we are asked about and told about in the problem are connected

We proceed as in previous examples.

Step 3: Calculation of "Known" Moles

"Known" substance is I^-

$$\text{number of moles} = \text{concentration} \times \text{number of litres}$$
$$= \quad 0·2 \quad \times \quad 0·02$$
$$= \textbf{0·004 mol of } I^-$$

Step 4: Calculation of "Unknown" Moles

From the Mole Statement:

1 mol of MnO_4^- reacts with 5 mol of I^-

Reversing to put MnO_4^- on the right hand side, we have:

5 mol of I^- reacts with 1 mol of MnO_4^-

1 mol of I^- reacts with $\dfrac{1}{5}$ mol of MnO_4^-

0·004 mol of I^- reacts with $\dfrac{0·004}{5}$ mol of MnO_4^-

= **0·0008 mol of MnO_4^-**

Step 5: Finishing Off

$$\text{volume (in litres)} = \frac{\text{number of moles}}{\text{concentration}}$$

$$= \frac{0·0008}{0·064}$$

$$= \textbf{0·0125 } l \textbf{ (12·5 cm}^3\textbf{)}$$

PROBLEMS 15.31 – 15.40

These problems involve redox reactions of the type illustrated in Worked Example 15.4

15.31

$$Cr_2O_7^{2-} + 14H^+ + 6e^- \longrightarrow 2Cr^{3+} + 7H_2O$$
$$SO_3^{2-} + H_2O \longrightarrow SO_4^{2-} + 2H^+ + 2e^-$$

The above ion-electron equations represent the reduction and oxidation reactions which take place when a solution of dichromate ions, $Cr_2O_7^{2-}$, in acid solution react with sulphite ions, SO_3^{2-}.

What volume of a 0·05 mol l^{-1} solution of dichromate ions would react with 30 cm^3 of a 0·25 mol l^{-1} solution of sulphite ions?

15.32

$$MnO_4^- + 8H^+ + 5e^- \longrightarrow Mn^{2+} + 4H_2O$$
$$2Cl^- \longrightarrow Cl_2 + 2e^-$$

What volume of a 0·24 mol l^{-1} solution of acidified permanganate ions would exactly react with 120 cm^3 of a 0·16 mol l^{-1} solution of chloride ions?

15.33

$$I_2 + 2e^- \longrightarrow 2I^-$$
$$2S_2O_3^{2-} \longrightarrow S_4O_6^{2-} + 2e^-$$

25 cm^3 of a 0·05 mol l^{-1} solution of thiosulphate ions, $2S_2O_3^{2-}$, reacts exactly with 10 cm^3 of a solution of I_2. What concentration is the solution?

15.34
$$Fe^{3+} + e^- \longrightarrow Fe^{2+}$$
$$SO_3^{2-} + H_2O \longrightarrow SO_4^{2-} + 2H^+ + 2e^-$$

25 cm^3 of a solution containing 0·016 mol l^{-1} sulphite ions is titrated with 0·02 mol l^{-1} Fe^{3+} solution. What volume of the Fe^{3+} solution would be required to obtain the exact end-point of this titration?

15.35
$$2BrO_3^- + 12H^+ + 10e^- \longrightarrow Br_2 + 6H_2O$$
$$2I^- \longrightarrow I_2 + 2e^-$$

32 cm^3 of a 0·0125 mol l^{-1} solution of bromate ions, BrO$_3^-$, exactly oxidises 25 cm^3 of a solution of iodide ions. What is the concentration of the iodide ion solution?

15.36
$$2HClO + 2H^+ + 2e^- \longrightarrow Cl_2 + 2H_2O$$
$$2I^- \longrightarrow I_2 + 2e^-$$

25 cm^3 of a 0·02 mol l^{-1} solution of hypochlorous acid, HClO, is exactly reduced by 10 cm^3 of a solution of iodide ions. What is the concentration of the iodide ion solution?

15.37
$$Fe^{3+} + e^- \longrightarrow Fe^{2+}$$
$$SO_3^{2-} + H_2O \longrightarrow SO_4^{2-} + 2H^+ + 2e^-$$

12·8 cm^3 of a 0·12 mol l^{-1} solution of sulphite ions is exactly oxidised by 7·68 cm^3 of a solution of iron(III) ions. What is the concentration of the iron(III) ions present?

15.38
$$Cr_2O_7^{2-} + 14H^+ + 6e^- \longrightarrow Cr^{3+} + 7H_2O$$
$$Fe^{2+} \longrightarrow Fe^{3+} + e^-$$

40 cm^3 of a solution containing acidified dichromate ions with a concentration of 0·015 mol l^{-1} is titrated with 0·2 mol l^{-1} Fe^{2+} solution. What volume of the Fe^{2+} solution would be required to obtain the exact end-point of this titration?

15.39
$$(COOH)_2 \longrightarrow 2CO_2 + 2H^+ + 2e^-$$
$$MnO_4^- + 8H^+ + 5e^- \longrightarrow Mn^{2+} + 4H_2O$$

A 0·01 mol l^{-1} solution of oxalic acid, (COOH)$_2$, is titrated against 16 cm^3 of an acidified solution containing 0·005 mol l^{-1} permanganate ions until the end point is reached. What volume of oxalic acid solution must have reacted?

15.40
$$H_2O_2 + 2H^+ + 2e^- \longrightarrow 2H_2O$$
$$Fe^{2+} \longrightarrow Fe^{3+} + e^-$$

10 cm^3 of a 2·4 mol l^{-1} solution of hydrogen peroxide, H$_2$O$_2$, is titrated with a solution containing 1·25 mol l^{-1} of Fe^{2+}. What volume of the Fe^{2+} solution will be required to react exactly with the hydrogen peroxide?

16. CALCULATIONS FROM EQUATIONS — 3

In this chapter, we consider calculations from equations where the only chemical species we are concerned with are gases under the same conditions of temperature and pressure, and where the quantities of gas are expressed as **volumes**. Because a mole of **any gas** occupies the same volume under the same conditions, we do not have to calculate actual numbers of moles in this type of problem; we simply use the volumes of gases since these values are proportional to the numbers of moles.

WORKED EXAMPLE 16.1

What volume of carbon dioxide would be produced if 20 cm^3 of ethane is burned in an excess of oxygen? (All volumes measured under the same conditions of temperature and pressure.)

We start the problem as in previous calculations from equations:

Step 1:   Balanced Equation

$$C_2H_6\,(g) \quad + \quad 3\tfrac{1}{2}O_2\,(g) \quad \longrightarrow \quad 2CO_2\,(g) \quad + \quad 3H_2O\,(l)$$

Step 2:   Mole Statement

       1 mole of C_2H_6 will produce 2 mol of CO_2

Step 3:   Volume Statement

Since 1 mol of **any gas** occupies the same volume under the same conditions of temperature and pressure, we can rewrite our mole statement in terms of "volumes" as below, where the "volumes" can be in any unit of volume provided that the same unit is used consistently throughout the problem:

       1 volume of C_2H_6 will produce 2 volumes of CO_2

Step 4:   Finishing Off

From the volume statement above, we can say that since:

       1 volume of C_2H_6 will produce 2 volumes of CO_2,

       20 cm^3 of C_2H_6 will produce **40 cm^3 of CO_2**

WORKED EXAMPLE 16.2

What would be the volume and composition of the resulting gas mixture if 100 cm^3 of butane was exploded in 800 cm^3 of oxygen? (All volumes are measured at 20 °C and at 1 atmosphere pressure.)

Step 1:   Balanced Equation

$$C_4H_{10}\,(g)\quad+\quad 6\tfrac{1}{2}O_2\,(g)\quad\longrightarrow\quad 4CO_2\,(g)\quad+\quad 5H_2O\,(l)$$

Steps 2 and 3:   Mole and Volume Statements

The problem refers to the volumes of **gases**; at 20 °C and 1 atmosphere pressure (roughly room conditions), water is a liquid and all the other species in the equation are gases, as indicated by the use of the "state subscripts" (l and g) in the equation. We therefore ignore the quantity of water involved since the problem only asks about the resulting **gas mixture**) and write statements as below.

1 mole   of C_4H_{10} will react with $6\tfrac{1}{2}$ mol   of O_2 to form 4 mol   of CO_2

1 volume of C_4H_{10} will react with $6\tfrac{1}{2}$ volumes of O_2 to form 4 volumes of CO_2

Step 4:   Finishing Off

Consideration of the volume statement and the available volumes of butane and oxygen tells us that there is more oxygen present than will react (it is in excess). All 100 cm^3 of butane will react as follows:

1 volume of C_4H_{10} will react with $6\tfrac{1}{2}$ volumes of O_2 to form 4 volumes of CO_2,

100 cm^3 of C_4H_{10} will react with 650 cm^3 of O_2 to form 400 cm^3 of CO_2.

Thus the final mixutre will contain **400 cm^3 of CO_2**. Since we started with 800 cm^3 of oxygen but only 650 cm^3 of it has reacted, there will also be **150 cm^3 of O_2** unreacted in the final gas mixture.

PROBLEMS 16.1 – 16.10

These problems involve gases measured under the same conditions of temperature and pressure and should be worked out by the method described in Worked Examples 16.1 and 16.2.

16. 1 $CH_4\,(g)\quad+\quad 2O_2\,(g)\quad\longrightarrow\quad CO_2\,(g)\quad+\quad 2H_2O\,(l)$

100 cm^3 of methane is exploded with 300 cm^3 of oxygen.

(a)   Which gas is in excess?

(b)   What is the volume and composition of the resulting gas mixture?

16. 2 $CO\,(g)\quad+\quad \tfrac{1}{2}O_2\,(g)\quad\longrightarrow\quad CO_2\,(g)$

50 cm^3 of carbon monoxide is burned with 20 cm^3 of oxygen.

(a)   Which gas is in excess?

(b)   What is the volume and composition of the resulting gas mixture?

16. 3 $$C_3H_8\,(g)\ +\ 5O_2\,(g)\ \longrightarrow\ 3CO_2\,(g)\ +\ 4H_2O\,(l)$$

20 l of propane is burned in 140 l of oxygen. Calculate the volume and composition of the resulting gas mixture.

16. 4 $$C_3H_6\,(g)\ +\ 4\tfrac{1}{2}O_2\,(g)\ \longrightarrow\ 3CO_2\,(g)\ +\ 3H_2O\,(l)$$

400 l of cyclopropane is exploded with 5000 l of oxygen. Calculate the volume and composition of the resulting gas mixture.

16. 5 $$C_2H_6\,(g)\ +\ 3\tfrac{1}{2}O_2\,(g)\ \longrightarrow\ 2CO_2\,(g)\ +\ 3H_2O\,(g)$$

200 cm^3 of ethane is burned completely in 2 l of oxygen. Calculate the volume and composition of the resulting gas mixture if all volume measurements were made at a temperature of 200 °C and a pressure of 1 atmosphere; i.e. under conditions where water is in the gas state (steam).

16. 6 $$N_2H_4\,(g)\ +\ O_2\,(g)\ \longrightarrow\ N_2\,(g)\ +\ 2H_2O\,(g)$$

100 l of hydrazine, N_2H_4, is burned in 400 l of oxygen to form nitrogen gas and steam. What will the volume and composition of the resulting gas mixture be if all measurements were taken at 300 °C and at the same pressure?

16. 7 $$C_4H_{10}\,(g)\ +\ 6\tfrac{1}{2}O_2\,(g)\ \longrightarrow\ 4CO_2\,(g)\ +\ 5H_2O\,(l)$$

150 l of butane is burned in 2000 l of oxygen. What is the volume and composition of the resulting gas mixture? (All volume measurements taken at a temperature of 20 °C and 1 atmosphere pressure.)

16. 8 $$C_6H_{14}\,(g)\ +\ 6H_2O\,(g)\ \longrightarrow\ 6CO_2\,(g)\ +\ 13H_2\,(g)$$

Hydrogen can be obtained from hexane by catalytic reaction with steam. Under certain conditions, 4×10^4 l of hexane is reacted with an excess of steam. Assuming the reaction goes to completion, calculate the volume of (a) carbon dioxide and (b) hydrogen produced.

16. 9 $$CS_2\,(g)\ +\ 3Cl_2\,(g)\ \longrightarrow\ CCl_4\,(g)\ +\ S_2Cl_2\,(g)$$

Tetrachloromethane, CCl_4, can be made industrially by the above process in which carbon disulphide is reacted with chlorine gas. Under certain conditions, 5×10^5 l of carbon disulphide gas is reacted completely in the presence of $2{\cdot}5 \times 10^6$ l of chlorine. What is the composition by volume of the resulting gas mixture?

16.10 $$C_6H_{14}\,(g)\ +\ 3O_2\,(g)\ \longrightarrow\ 6CO\,(g)\ +\ 7H_2\,(g)$$

Hexane can be partially oxidised to carbon monoxide and oxygen gases. Under certain conditions, $3{\cdot}15 \times 10^6$ l of hydrogen gas was obtained from this reaction. What volume of gaseous hexane, measured under the same conditions, must have reacted?

17. CALCULATIONS FROM EQUATIONS — 4

In this chapter we consider calculations from equations involving the molar volumes and densities of gases. The work of Chapter 4 should be revised before continuing.

WORKED EXAMPLE 17.1

8.8×10^3 kg of propane is completely burned in an excess of oxygen. What volume of carbon dioxide would be produced if its density under these conditions is 2 g l^{-1}

Step 1:   Balanced Equation

$$C_3H_8 \; + \; 5O_2 \longrightarrow 3CO_2 \; + \; 4H_2O$$

Step 2:   Mole Statement

> 1 mole of C_3H_8 produces 3 mol of CO_2

Step 3:   Calculation of "Known" Moles

The known material is propane. Although its mass is given as 8.8×10^3 kg, it is easier at this stage to assume that we have 8.8 g of the substance and convert to kg at the end of the problem. (See Worked Example 14.2 and the examples following in Chapter 14.)

$$
\begin{aligned}
44 \text{ g} &= 1 \quad \text{mol of } C_3H_8 \\
1 \text{ g} &= \frac{1}{44} \text{ mol of } C_3H_8 \\
8.8 \text{ g} &= \frac{8.8}{44} \text{ mol of } C_3H_8 \\
&= 0.2 \text{ mol of } C_3H_8
\end{aligned}
$$

Step 4:   Calculation of "Unknown" Moles

> 1   mol of C_3H_8 produces   3 mol of CO_2
>
> 0.2 mol of C_3H_8 produces 0.2×3 mol of CO_2
>
> **= 0.6 mol of CO_2**

Step 5:   Finishing Off

We have calculated that:

> 8.8 g of C_3H_8 would produce 0.6 mol of CO_2

We have to obtain the **volume** of CO_2 and are given that the density of the gas is 2 g l^{-1} under the conditions of the reaction.

We convert the 0.6 mol of CO_2 into grams:

$$
\begin{aligned}
1 \quad \text{mol of } CO_2 &= 44 \text{ g} \\
0.6 \text{ mol of } CO_2 &= 0.6 \times 44 \text{ g} \\
&= 26.4 \text{ g}
\end{aligned}
$$

Using the density figure, we have:

$$2 \text{ g of } CO_2 \text{ has a volume of} \quad 1 \quad l$$

$$1 \text{ g of } CO_2 \text{ has a volume of} \quad \frac{1}{2} \quad l$$

$$26{\cdot}4 \text{ g of } CO_2 \text{ has a volume of} \quad \frac{26{\cdot}4}{2} \quad l$$

$$= \quad \mathbf{13{\cdot}2} \ l$$

This is the volume of CO_2 that would be given off if $8{\cdot}8$ g of C_3H_8 had reacted. However, the **actual** mass of C_3H_8 was $8{\cdot}8 \times 10^3$ kg. We proceed as follows:

$$8{\cdot}8 \qquad \text{g} \quad \text{of } C_3H_8 \text{ produces} \quad 13{\cdot}2 \qquad l \text{ of } CO_2$$

$$8{\cdot}8 \qquad \text{kg} \quad \text{of } C_3H_8 \text{ produces} \quad 13{\cdot}2 \times 10^3 \qquad l \text{ of } CO_2$$
$$\text{(since 1 kg} = 10^3 \text{ g)}$$

$$8{\cdot}8 \times 10^3 \quad \text{kg} \quad \text{of } C_3H_8 \text{ produces} \quad 13{\cdot}2 \times 10^3 \times 10^3 \, l \text{ of } CO_2$$

$$13{\cdot}2 \times 10^6 \qquad l \text{ of } CO_2$$

$$= \quad \mathbf{1{\cdot}32 \times 10^7} \qquad \mathbf{\textit{l} \text{ of } CO_2}$$

WORKED EXAMPLE 17.2

Under certain conditions, the molar volume of carbon dioxide is 30 l. What volume of carbon dioxide would be produced, under these conditions, by the addition of 5·3 g of sodium carbonate to 600 cm^3 of 0·4 mol l^{-1} hydrochloric acid?

Step 1:   Balanced Equation

$$Na_2CO_3 \ + \ 2HCl \ \longrightarrow \ 2NaCl \ + \ H_2O \ + \ CO_2$$

Step 2:   Mole Statement

$$1 \text{ mole of } Na_2CO_3 \text{ produces 1 mol of } CO_2$$

Step 3:   Calculation of "Known" Moles

Since we are told about both reactants, we work out the number of moles of each to identify which one is in excess, i.e. which one we have too much of. (See Worked Example 15.3 in Chapter 15 if this is unfamiliar.)

Na_2CO_3

$$106 \ \text{ g of } Na_2CO_3 \ = \ 1 \ \text{mol}$$

$$1 \ \text{ g of } Na_2CO_3 \ = \ \frac{1}{106} \text{ mol}$$

$$5{\cdot}3 \text{ g of } Na_2CO_3 \ = \ \frac{5{\cdot}3}{106} \text{ mol}$$

$$= \quad \mathbf{0{\cdot}05 \ mol}$$

HCl

$$\text{number of moles} = \text{concentration} \times \text{volume (in litres)}$$

$$= \quad 0\cdot4 \quad \times \quad 0\cdot6$$

$$= \quad \textbf{0·24 mol}$$

So we have 0·05 mol of Na_2CO_3 and 0·24 mol of HCl. Looking at the balanced equation, we see that 1 mol of Na_2CO_3 will react with 2 mol of HCl. Since we only have 0·05 mol of Na_2CO_3, it can only react with 0·1 mol of HCl; the excess (left over) HCl will not react. **So we take the 0·05 mol of Na_2CO_3 for our "known" moles since we know that all of this quantity will react.**

Step 4:   Calculation of "Unknown" Moles

From the statement we have:

$$1 \quad \text{mol of } Na_2CO_3 \text{ produces 1} \quad \text{mol of } CO_2$$

$$0\cdot05 \text{ mol of } Na_2CO_3 \text{ produces } \textbf{0·05 mol of } CO_2$$

Step 5:   Finishing Off

We are asked for the volume of CO_2 under the conditions where the molar volume of the gas is 30 l. This simply means that the volume of 1 mol of the gas is 30 l under these conditions.

$$1 \quad \text{mol of } CO_2 \text{ has a volume of} \quad 30\ l$$

$$0\cdot05 \text{ mol of } CO_2 \text{ has a volume of } 0\cdot05 \times 30\ l$$

$$= \textbf{1·5}\ l$$

PROBLEMS 17.1 – 17.10

These problems are of the types illustrated in Worked Examples 17.1 and 17.2, involving gas densities and volumes.

17. 1 $$CH_4\,(g) \ + \ 2O_2\,(g) \ \longrightarrow \ CO_2\,(g) \ + \ 2H_2O\,(l)$$

7·2 g of methane is burned completely in oxygen according to the above equation. What volume of carbon dioxide would be produced if the molar volume of this gas is 200 l under these conditions?

17. 2 $$Na_2CO_3\,(s) \ + \ 2HCl\,(aq) \ \longrightarrow \ 2NaCl\,(aq) \ + \ CO_2\,(g) \ + \ H_2O\,(l)$$

5·3 g of sodium carbonate is reacted with an excess of dilute hydrochloric acid. What volume of carbon dioxide will be given off if the density of the gas is 2 g l^{-1}?

17. 3 $$4NH_3\,(g) \ + \ 5O_2\,(g) \ \longrightarrow \ 4NO\,(g) \ + \ 6H_2O\,(l)$$

400 l of oxygen is used up in the above reaction, measured under conditions in which its density is 1·6 g l^{-1}. What mass of ammonia must have reacted?

17. 4 $$3F_2\,(g) \ + \ 3H_2O\,(g) \ \longrightarrow \ 6HF\,(g) \ + \ O_3\,(g)$$

1824 g of fluorine is reacted completely with an excess of steam. What volume of ozone gas, O_3, would be produced under conditions where its density is 2·4 g l^{-1}?

17. 5 $Zn\,(s)\ +\ 2HCl\,(aq)\ \longrightarrow\ ZnCl_2\,(aq)\ +\ H_2\,(g)$

Under certain conditions, the molar volume of hydrogen gas is 24 l. What mass of zinc would be required to react with an excess of hydrochloric acid to produce 0·96 l of hydrogen under these conditions?

17. 6 $H_2SO_4\,(aq)\ +\ CaCO_3\,(s)\ \longrightarrow\ CaSO_4\,(aq)\ +\ CO_2\,(g)\ +\ H_2O\,(l)$

What volume of carbon dioxide would be given off when 20 g of calcium carbonate is completely reacted with an excess of sulphuric acid? The molar volume of carbon dioxide is 22 l under the reaction conditions.

17. 7 $N_2H_4\,(g)\ +\ 2F_2\,(g)\ \longrightarrow\ N_2\,(g)\ +\ 4HF\,(g)$

What volume of hydrogen fluoride would be produced by the complete reaction of 6·4 kg of hydrazine, N_2H_4, with an excess of fluorine? The molar volume of hydrogen fluoride is 50 l under the conditions of measurement.

17. 8 $Fe_2O_3\,(s)\ +\ 3CO\,(g)\ \longrightarrow\ 2Fe\,(s)\ +\ 3CO_2\,(g)$

Under conditions in which the molar volume of carbon dioxide is 125 l, $1·875 \times 10^5$ l of the gas is obtained by the reduction of iron(III) oxide by carbon monoxide. What mass of iron(III) oxide must have been reduced?

17. 9 $3Cu\,(s)\ +\ 8HNO_3\,(aq)\ \longrightarrow\ 3Cu(NO_3)_2\,(aq)\ +\ 4H_2O\,(l)\ +\ 2NO\,(g)$

15·36 g of copper is completely reacted with an excess of nitric acid according to the above equation. Assuming that this is the only reaction taking place, calculate the volume of nitrogen monoxide which would be evolved if its density under the reaction conditions is 1·6 g l^{-1}.

17.10 $C_6H_{14}\,(g)\ +\ 6H_2O\,(l)\ \longrightarrow\ 6CO\,(g)\ +\ 13H_2\,(g)$

$1·08 \times 10^6$ l of hexane is reacted with an excess of steam according to the above equation. If the molar volume of the hexane under these conditions is 120 l, calculate the mass of hydrogen which would be produced.

18.   CALCULATIONS FROM EQUATIONS — 5

This chapter uses the same method as that described in earlier chapters to solve calculations from chemical equations, but involving the use of the Avogadro Constant. The work of Chapter 5 should be revised before proceeding.

WORKED EXAMPLE 18.1

150 cm^3 of dilute sulphuric acid reacts completely with an excess of sodium carbonate; in the process, $1 \cdot 806 \times 10^{21}$ molecules of carbon dioxide are given off. What was the concentration of the acid?

Step 1:   Balanced Equation

$$H_2SO_4 + Na_2CO_3 \longrightarrow Na_2SO_4 + H_2O + CO_2$$

Step 2:   Mole Statement

1 mole of H_2SO_4 produces 1 mol of CO_2

Step 3:   Calculation of "Known" Moles

$6 \cdot 02 \times 10^{23}$ molecules of CO_2 =   1   mol of CO_2

1   molecule of CO_2 = $\dfrac{1}{6 \cdot 02 \times 10^{23}}$ mol of CO_2

$1 \cdot 806 \times 10^{21}$ molecules of CO_2 = $\dfrac{1 \cdot 806 \times 10^{21}}{6 \cdot 02 \times 10^{23}}$ mol of CO_2

= 3×10^{-3} **mol of CO_2**

Step 4:   Calculation of "Unknown" Moles

1 mol of H_2SO_4 produces 1 mol of CO_2

Rearranging this statement to make our answer come out on the right hand side of the problem we have:

1   mol of CO_2 is produced by   1 mol of H_2SO_4

3×10^{-3} mol of CO_2 is produced by **3×10^{-3} mol of H_2SO_4**

Step 5:   Finishing Off

concentration (molarity)   = $\dfrac{\text{no. of moles}}{\text{no. of litres}}$

= $\dfrac{3 \times 10^{-3}}{0 \cdot 15}$ mol l^{-1}

=   **$0 \cdot 02$ mol l^{-1}**

PROBLEMS 18.1 – 18.15

These problems involve the use of the Avogadro Constant, 6.02×10^{23}.

18. 1 $\qquad$ $C_3H_8 + 5O_2 \longrightarrow 3CO_2 + 4H_2O$

0.11 g of propane is burned completely in excess oxygen. How many molecules of *(a)* water and *(b)* carbon dioxide will be produced?

18. 2 $\qquad$ $2Na + 2H_2O \longrightarrow 2NaOH + H_2$

3.68 g of sodium is completely reacted with water. How many molecules of hydrogen will be given off in the process?

18. 3 $\qquad$ $C_2H_4 + Br_2 \longrightarrow C_2H_4Br_2$

2.24 g of ethene is completely brominated by reaction with an excess of bromine gas. How many atoms of bromine would have reacted?

18. 4 $\qquad$ $Ca(OH)_2 + CO_2 \longrightarrow CaCO_3 + H_2O$

1.505×10^{21} molecules of carbon dioxide react with calcium hydroxide solution, causing a precipitate of calcium carbonate to form. What mass should the precipitate be after filtering and drying?

18. 5 $\qquad$ $H_2O_2 + Au_2O_3 \longrightarrow 2Au + 2O_2 + H_2O$

1.36 g of hydrogen peroxide, H_2O_2, is completely reacted with gold(III) oxide forming a precipitate of gold, evolving oxygen gas and producing water. Calculate the number of gold atoms precipitated.

18. 6 $\qquad$ $2Fe_2O_3 + 3C \longrightarrow 4Fe + 3CO_2$

6.4 g of iron(III) oxide is completely reduced by carbon to carbon dioxide. How many atoms of carbon have reacted?

18. 7 $\qquad$ $2NaOH + H_2SO_4 \longrightarrow Na_2SO_4 + 2H_2O$

1.6 g of sodium hydroxide is reacted with an excess of sulphuric acid. How many molecules of water will have been produced during the reaction?

18. 8 $\qquad$ $C_6H_{12}O_6 + 6O_2 \longrightarrow 6CO_2 + 6H_2O$

1.806×10^{20} molecules of glucose are completely burned in an excess of oxygen. What mass of carbon dioxide would be produced?

18. 9 $\qquad$ $2NH_3 + H_2SO_4 \longrightarrow (NH_4)_2SO_4$

2.408×10^{21} molecules of ammonia exactly neutralise a 50 cm^3 solution of sulphuric acid. What was the concentration of the acid?

18.10 $\qquad$ $CH_3CHO + 3Cl_2 \longrightarrow CCl_3CHO + 3HCl$

5.418×10^{24} molecules of Cl_2 react completely with ethanal, CH_3CHO. What mass of trichloroethanal would be formed?

18.11 $\qquad$ $C_2H_2 + 2H_2 \longrightarrow C_2H_6$

A sample of ethyne, C_2H_2, is completely hydrogenated to form ethane by the addition of 2.408×10^{20} molecules of hydrogen gas. What mass of ethane would be produced?

18.12
$$3NO_2 + H_2O \longrightarrow 2HNO_3 + NO$$

How many molecules of nitrogen dioxide would be required to form 5·04 g of nitric acid by the process described by the above equation?

18.13
$$2Ag_2CO_3 \longrightarrow 4Ag + 2CO_2 + O_2$$

What mass of silver(I) carbonate would completely decompose by the above equation to form $7·525 \times 10^{22}$ atoms of silver?

18.14
$$2HCl + Na_2CO_3 \longrightarrow 2NaCl + CO_2 + H_2O$$

$9·632 \times 10^{22}$ molecules of hydrogen chloride gas are completely dissolved in water. This solution is then added to 200 cm^3 of a 1 mol l^{-1} solution of sodium carbonate.

(a) Which reactant is in excess? (Refer back to Worked Example 15.3 of Chapter 15 if unsure.)

(b) How many molecules of carbon dioxide will be evolved during the reaction?

18.15
$$Mg + 2CH_3COOH \longrightarrow Mg(CH_3COO)_2 + H_2$$

0·48 g of magnesium was added to 250 cm^3 of a 0·2 mol l^{-1} solution of ethanoic acid.

(a) Which reactant is in excess?

(b) How many molecules of hydrogen gas will have been given off during the reaction?

APPENDIX 1

Table of Relative Atomic Masses

Element	Symbol	RAM	Element	Symbol	RAM
Aluminium	Al	27	Magnesium	Mg	24
Argon	Ar	40	Mercury	Hg	201
Barium	Ba	137	Neon	Ne	20
Bromine	Br	80	Nickel	Ni	59
Calcium	Ca	40	Nitrogen	N	14
Carbon	C	12	Oxygen	O	16
Chlorine	Cl	35·5	Phosphorus	P	31
Chromium	Cr	52	Platinum	Pt	195
Cobalt	Co	59	Potassium	K	39
Copper	Cu	64	Silicon	Si	28
Fluorine	F	19	Silver	Ag	108
Gold	Au	197	Sodium	Na	23
Helium	He	4	Sulphur	S	32
Hydrogen	H	1	Tin	Sn	119
Iodine	I	127	Titanium	Ti	48
Iron	Fe	56	Vanadium	V	51
Krypton	Kr	84	Xenon	Xe	131
Lead	Pb	207	Zinc	Zn	65
Lithium	Li	7			

APPENDIX 2

Enthalpies of Formation and Combustion of Selected Substances

Substance	Standard enthalpy of formation kJ mol^{-1}	Standard enthalpy of combustion kJ mol^{-1}
hydrogen	—	−286
carbon (graphite)	—	−394
sulphur (rhombic)	—	−297
methane	−75	−882
ethane	−85	−1542
propane	−104	−2202
butane	−125	−2877
benzene	49	−3273
ethene	52	−1387
ethyne	227	−1305
methanol	−239	−715
ethanol	−278	−1371
propan-1-ol	—	−2010
methanoic acid	−409	−263
ethanoic acid	−487	−876

Selected Bond and Mean Bond Enthalpies

Bond Enthalpies

Bond	Enthalpy /kJ mol^{-1}
H — H	436
O = O	497
N ≡ N	949
F — F	155
Cl — Cl	243
Br — Br	194
I — I	161
H — F	569
H — Cl	431
H — Br	366
H — I	299

Mean Bond Enthalpies

Bond	Mean Enthalpy /kJ mol^{-1}
Si — Si	200
C — C	337
C = C	607
C ≡ C	828
C ⋯ C (aromatic)	519
H — O	458
H — N	387
C — H	414
C — O	331
C = O	724
C — F	486
C — Cl	326
C — Br	280
C — I	239

Enthalpy of Sublimation of Carbon

The energy required to convert 1 mole solid carbon into 1 mole gaseous carbon is 715 kJ at 298 K. The equation in C (s) → C (g)   ΔH = 715 kJ

APPENDIX 3

Ionisation Energies of Selected Elements

Element	Symbol	Ionisation Energies kJ mol^{-1}			
		First	Second	Third	Fourth
hydrogen	H	1320	—	—	—
helium	He	2380	5260	—	—
lithium	Li	526	7310	11800	—
beryllium	Be	905	1770	14800	—
boron	B	807	2440	3660	25000
carbon	C	1090	2360	4640	6220
nitrogen	N	1410	2860	4580	7470
oxygen	O	1320	3400	5320	7470
fluorine	F	1690	3380	6060	8410
neon	Ne	2090	3960	6140	9360
sodium	Na	502	4560	6920	9540
magnesium	Mg	744	1460	7750	10500
aluminium	Al	584	1830	2760	11600
silicon	Si	792	1590	3250	4350
phosphorus	P	1020	1920	2930	4950
sulphur	S	1010	2260	3380	4560
chlorine	Cl	1260	2310	3840	5160
argon	Ar	1530	2670	3950	5770
potassium	K	425	3060	4440	5880
calcium	Ca	596	1160	4930	6470
scandium	Sc	637	1250	2410	7130
titanium	Ti	664	1320	2670	4170
vanadium	V	656	1430	2850	4600
chromium	Cr	659	1600	3000	4800
manganese	Mn	723	1520	3270	5000
iron	Fe	766	1570	2970	5480
cobalt	Co	764	1660	3250	—
nickel	Ni	743	1770	3410	5400
copper	Cu	751	1970	3570	5700
zinc	Zn	913	1740	3850	5990
arsenic	As	953	1800	2750	4830
bromine	Br	1150	2100	3480	4560
rubidium	Rb	409	2670	3880	—
strontium	Sr	556	1080	4120	5500
silver	Ag	737	2080	3380	—
tin	Sn	715	1420	2960	3930
antimony	Sb	816	1610	2460	4260
iodine	I	1020	1850	2040	—
caesium	Cs	382	2440	—	—
barium	Ba	509	979	3420	—
gold	Au	896	1990	—	—
lead	Pb	722	1460	3100	4080

Notes: The first ionisation energy for an element E refers to the reaction $E(g) \rightarrow E^+(g) + e^-$; the second ionisation energy refers to $E^+(g) \rightarrow E^{2+}(g) + e^-$; etc.

APPENDIX 4:

Definitions of Enthalpy Terms

Below are noted the names and definitions of the enthalpy terms used in Chapters 9 to 12. Particular attention should be paid to the use of state scripts (s, l, g, aq) in equations, since they are often essential in describing the processes. They are listed in alphabetical order of the *main* word which describes the process.

BOND ENTHALPY

The Bond Enthalpy of a covalent bond is the energy which requires to be put in to break one mole of the bond in the gas state. Many Bond Enthalpies are described as **Mean** Bond Enthalpies, meaning that they are **average** values of the bond enthalpy taken from different compounds containing the same bond.

The equation and ΔH representing the Bond Enthalpy of the Cl — Cl bond are shown below.

$$Cl_2 (g) \longrightarrow 2Cl (g) \qquad\qquad \Delta H = +243 \text{ kJ mol}^{-1}$$

The equation and ΔH value represent 4 × the Bond Enthalpy of C — H.

$$CH_4 (g) \longrightarrow C (g) + 4H (g) \qquad\qquad \Delta H = +1656 \text{ kJ mol}^{-1}$$

That is, the Bond Enthalpy of C — H is 414 kJ mol^{-1}.

As defined, these are **bond breaking** processes which are **endothermic**. **Bond making** processes are described by the reverse equations and are, of course, **exothermic**.

ENTHALPY OF COMBUSTION

The Enthalpy of Combustion (often abbreviated ΔH_c) of a substance is the amount of energy given out when 1 mole of the substance is burned in an excess of oxygen. All substances are considered to be at their usual, room temperature, states, e.g. water as a liquid, oxygen as a gas, etc.

By definition, all combustions are exothermic and therefore have negative ΔH values.

The equation and ΔH value representing the Enthalpy of Combustion of methane is given below.

$$CH_4 (g) + 2O_2 (g) \longrightarrow CO_2 (g) + 2H_2O (l) \qquad\qquad \Delta H = -890 \text{ kJ mol}^{-1}$$

ELECTRON GAIN ENTHALPY (or Electron Affinity)

The Electron Gain Enthalpy of an element is the amount of energy given out when 1 mole of **gaseous atoms** gain 1 mole of electrons to form 1 mole of singly-charged negative ions. Note that this process is **always exothermic**. The equation and ΔH value representing the Electron Gain Enthalpy of chlorine are shown below..

$$Cl (g) + e^- \longrightarrow Cl^- (g) \qquad\qquad \Delta H = -350 \text{ kJ mol}^{-1}$$

There exist values for Second Electron Gain Enthalpies which refer to the addition of a **second** mole of electrons but we are unlikely to encounter them in this course.

Many text books use the term Electron Affinity instead of Electron Gain Enthalpy; the terms are identical in meaning.

ENTHALPY OF FORMATION

The Enthalpy of Formation (often abbreviated ΔH_f) of a compound is the amount of energy given out or taken in during the formation of 1 mole of the substance from its elements in their room temperature states. The equation and ΔH value representing the Enthalpy of Formation of ethanol is given below.

$$2C\,(s) \ + \ 3H_2\,(g) \ + \ \tfrac{1}{2}O_2\,(g) \longrightarrow C_2H_5OH\,(l) \qquad \Delta H = -278 \text{ kJ mol}^{-1}$$

By definition, the Enthalpy of Formation of an **element** is zero. This may be understood by considering that the equation for the formation of oxygen from its elements (i.e. oxygen!) would be represented by the equation:

$$O_2\,(g) \longrightarrow O_2\,(g)$$

This, of course, is no change at all and therefore has a ΔH of zero.

ENTHALPY OF HYDRATION

The Enthalpy of Hydration of an ion is the energy given out when 1 mole of **gaseous** ions is dissolved completely in water. The equation and ΔH value representing the Enthalpy of Hydration of sodium ions are shown below.

$$Na^+\,(g) \longrightarrow Na^+\,(aq) \qquad \Delta H = -794 \text{ kJ mol}^{-1}$$

Note that hydration is **always exothermic**.

IONISATION ENTHALPY

The First Ionisation Enthalpy is the energy required to remove 1 mole of electrons from 1 mole of gaseous atoms to form 1 mole of gaseous, positive ions.

The Second Ionisation Enthalpy is the energy required to remove a **second** mole of electrons from 1 mole of single positive ions.

Third etc. Ionisation Enthalpies are similarly defined.

The First Ionisation Enthalpy of sodium is represented by the equation below.

$$Na\,(g) \longrightarrow Na^+\,(g) \ + \ e^- \qquad \Delta H = +502 \text{ kJ mol}^{-1}$$

The Second Ionisation Enthalpy of sodium is represented by the equation below.

$$Na^+\,(g) \longrightarrow Na^{2+}\,(g) \ + \ e^- \qquad \Delta H = +502 \text{ kJ mol}^{-1}$$

Note that this process is **always endothermic**, and always refers to the **removal of electrons** and the **formation of positive ions**, even when the element would more normally form a negative ion. So, for example, the First Ionisation Enthalpy of chlorine is represented by the equation and ΔH value below.

$$Cl\,(g) \longrightarrow Cl^+\,(g) \ + \ e^- \qquad \Delta H = +1260 \text{ kJ mol}^{-1}$$

ENTHALPY OF LATTICE BREAKING / MAKING

The Enthalpy of Lattice Breaking is the energy put in to break all the bonds in 1 mole of an ionic solid, converting all the ions into the gas state. The Enthalpy of Lattice Breaking of sodium chloride is represented by the equation and ΔH value below.

$$Na^+Cl^-\,(s) \longrightarrow Na^+\,(g) \ + \ Cl^-\,(g) \qquad \Delta H = +794 \text{ kJ mol}^{-1}$$

Lattice **Breaking** is **always exothermic**. The reverse process, Lattice **Making**, is simply the reverse process and is **always endothermic**. It is this latter process which usually appears in energy diagrams showing the formation of ionic compounds.

ENTHALPY OF NEUTRALISATION

The Enthalpy of Neutralisation is the heat given out when 1 mole of water is formed in the neutralisation of a strong acid and a strong alkali. Consider the two neutralisations below:

$$NaOH\,(aq) \; + \; HCl\,(aq) \longrightarrow NaCl\,(aq) \; + \; H_2O\,(l) \qquad \Delta H = -57\,kJ\,mol^{-1}$$

$$2NaOH\,(aq) \; + \; H_2SO_4\,(aq) \longrightarrow Na_2SO_4\,(aq) \; + \; 2H_2O\,(l) \qquad \Delta H = -114\,kJ\,mol^{-1}$$

In the first neutralisation the equation represents 1 mole of water being formed; in the second, two moles of water are formed. It can be seen that the ΔH in the second case is exactly twice that of the former; in each case, however, 57 kJ of heat is given out **for every mole of water formed**. Both equations, (and **all** equations representing strong acid – strong alkali neutralisations) can be described by the equation below, which has spectator ions omitted.

$$H^+\,(aq) \; + \; OH^-\,(aq) \longrightarrow H_2O\,(l) \qquad \Delta H = -57\,kJ\,mol^{-1}$$

(**Note:** The ΔH for the formation of 1 mole of water in a neutralisation which involves a **weak** acid or alkali is a **less negative** value than the figure quoted above. This is because some energy has to be **added** to the weak acid or alkali to cause it to break completely into its ions before the neutralisation can take place. When this energy **input** ($\Delta H+$) is added to the $-57\,kJ\,mol^{-1}$ for the neutralisation, an overall ΔH value which is less negative than $-57\,kJ\,mol^{-1}$ is obtained.

ENTHALPY OF SOLUTION

The Enthalpy of Solution of a substance is the amount of energy taken in or given out when 1 mole of the substance is dissolved completely in water. The equation and ΔH value representing the Enthalpy of Solution of sodium chloride are given below.

$$NaCl\,(s) \longrightarrow NaCl\,(aq) \qquad \Delta H = +4\,kJ\,mol^{-1}$$

This form of the equation does not show the charges on the ions; neither does it show that the ions in the solution are separate and free to move, while those in the solid are joined in a lattice. An alternative equation which shows this more clearly is:

$$Na^+Cl^-\,(s) \longrightarrow Na^+\,(aq) \; + \; Cl^-\,(aq) \qquad \Delta H = +4\,kJ\,mol^{-1}$$

Note that in neither equation was it necessary to include water since it is not actually changed during the process of dissolving.

ENTHALPY OF SUBLIMATION

The Enthalpy of Sublimation is the energy required to convert 1 mole of a solid element to the gas state. The most common example is the Enthalpy of Sublimation of carbon, represented by the equation and ΔH value below.

$$C\,(s) \longrightarrow C\,(g) \qquad \Delta H = +715\,kJ\,mol^{-1}$$

Note that the sublimation of **any** element is **always endothermic** (ΔH positive) since energy must always be **added** to break the bonds holding a solid together.

ANSWERS

CHAPTER 1 — Answers

Note that answers have been rounded to a maximum of three significant figures.

1. 1	6·93	**1. 2**	10·8	**1. 3**	39·1
1. 4	51·0	**1. 5**	80·0	**1. 6**	58·8
1. 7	28·1	**1. 8**	87·7	**1. 9**	91·3
1.10	40·0	**1.11**	184	**1.12**	140
1.13	55·9	**1.14**	207	**1.15**	107

CHAPTER 2 — Answers

Note: Answers are rounded, where necessary, to a maximum of 3 significant figures

2. 1	52·5 g	**2. 2**	0·02 mol	**2. 3**	1·2 mol
2. 4	8·55 g	**2. 5**	0·0025 mol	**2. 6**	53·6 g
2. 7	0·3 mol	**2. 8**	2·24 g	**2. 9**	0·015 mol
2.10	48 g	**2.11**	6·75 g	**2.12**	1·5 mol
2.13	3·84 g	**2.14**	0·14 mol	**2.15**	147 g
2.16	0·8 mol	**2.17**	150 g	**2.18**	0·12 mol
2.19	43·8 g	**2.20**	0·03 mol	**2.21**	0·2 mol l^{-1}
2.22	0·3 mol	**2.23**	0·2 mol l^{-1}	**2.24**	40 cm^3
2.25	0·15 mol	**2.26**	0·2 mol l^{-1}	**2.27**	250 cm^3
2.28	32 g	**2.29**	0·25 mol l^{-1}	**2.30**	1·32 g
2.31	1·5 l	**2.32**	40 cm^3	**2.33**	0·5 l
2.34	1·92 g	**2.35**	0·05 mol l^{-1}	**2.36**	0·05 mol l^{-1}
2.37	0·1 mol l^{-1}	**2.38**	0·96 g	**2.39**	0·2 mol l^{-1}
2.40	25 cm^3				

CHAPTER 3 — Answers

3. 1	SnO_2	**3. 2**	CH_4	**3. 3**	Mg_3N_2
3. 4	(a) C_2H_5 (b) C_4H_{10}	**3. 5**	(a) NO_2 (b) N_2O_4	**3. 6**	P_2O_5
3. 7	(a) Si_2H_5 (b) Si_4H_{10}	**3. 8**	(a) CH_2 (b) $C_{10}H_{20}$	**3. 9**	(a) $AlCl_3$ (b) Al_2Cl_6
3.10	Pb_3O_4	**3.11**	(a) CNH_4 (b) $C_2N_2H_8$	**3.12**	$Ca_3P_2O_8$
3.13	(a) CH_2O (b) $C_2H_4O_2$	**3.14**	$Na_2S_2O_3$	**3.15**	FeC_5O_5
3.16	$C_7O_2H_6$	**3.17**	$BaSO_3$	**3.18**	(a) C_2OH_4 (b) $C_4O_2H_8$
3.19	FeO_3H_3	**3.20**	(a) C_3H_2I (b) $C_6H_4I_2$	**3.21**	C_3H_4
3.22	C_3H_8O	**3.23**	(a) CH_2 (b) C_6H_{12}	**3.24**	$C_5H_{10}O$
3.25	(a) CH_2 (b) C_5H_{10}	**3.26**	C_2H_4O	**3.27**	$C_5H_{10}O_2$
3.28	$C_5H_{10}O_2$	**3.29**	$C_7H_{14}O_2$	**3.30**	$C_7H_6O_2$

CHAPTER 4 — Answers

NOTE: The answers below are given to a **maximum** of three significant figures.

4. 1 $22 \cdot 2 \, l$

4. 2 $1 \cdot 28 \, \text{g} \, l^{-1}$

4. 3 $N_2 \, 0 \cdot 237 \, l$; $H_2 \, 0 \cdot 234 \, l$

4. 4 $15 \cdot 9$

4. 5 $0 \cdot 523 \, \text{g} \, l^{-1}$

4. 6 $22 \cdot 2 \, l$

4. 7 $64 \cdot 0$

4. 8 $0 \cdot 52 \, \text{g} \, l^{-1}$

4. 9 $30 \cdot 0$; ethane, C_2H_6

4.10 $32 \cdot 1$; oxygen, O_2

4.11 $22 \cdot 4 \, l$

4.12 $0 \cdot 0236 \, \text{g}$

4.13 $3 \cdot 24 \, l$

4.14 $100 \, l$

4.15 $185 \, \text{g}$

4.16 $0 \cdot 045 \, l$

4.17 $24 \cdot 3 \, l$

4.18 SO_2: $1100 \, \text{g}$; O_2: $538 \, \text{g}$

4.19 $0 \cdot 0248 \, l$

4.20 $24 \cdot 3 \, l$

4.21   *(a)* $41 \cdot 2 \, l$;   *(b)* O_2: $0 \cdot 777 \, \text{g} \, l^{-1}$; CO_2: $1 \cdot 07 \, \text{g} \, l^{-1}$

4.22 $24 \, l$; $38 \cdot 0$

4.23 $15 \cdot 8$

4.24 $31 \cdot 7$

4·25 $0 \cdot 08 \, \text{g}$

CHAPTER 5 — Answers

The answers below are expressed to a **maximum** of 3 significant figures.

5. 1   *(a)* $6 \cdot 02 \times 10^{23}$; *(b)* $1 \cdot 20 \times 10^{24}$

5. 2   *(a)* $6 \cdot 02 \times 10^{23}$; *(b)* $1 \cdot 81 \times 10^{24}$

5. 3 $8 \cdot 43 \times 10^{24}$

5. 4 $0 \cdot 002$

5. 5 $0 \cdot 0375$

5. 6   *(a)* $2 \cdot 41 \times 10^{23}$; *(b)* $1 \cdot 20 \times 10^{23}$

5. 7 $4 \cdot 82 \times 10^{23}$

5. 8 $0 \cdot 6$

5. 9 $7 \cdot 22 \times 10^{23}$

5.10 $0 \cdot 04$

5.11 $1 \cdot 08 \times 10^{25}$

5.12 1×10^{-4}

5.13 $4 \cdot 06 \times 10^{24}$

5.14 2

5.15 $1 \cdot 81 \times 10^{24}$

5.16 $3 \cdot 33$

5.17 $4 \cdot 82 \times 10^{25}$

5.18 $2 \cdot 71 \times 10^{23}$

5.19 $8 \cdot 33 \times 10^{-6}$

5.20 $1 \cdot 44 \times 10^{23}$

5.21 $6 \cdot 02 \times 10^{21}$

5.22 $0 \cdot 3 \, \text{g}$

5.23 $1 \cdot 51 \times 10^{23}$

5.24 $0 \cdot 472 \, \text{g}$

5.25 $3 \cdot 27 \times 10^{-22} \, \text{g}$

5.26 $1 \cdot 20 \times 10^{23}$

5.27 $0 \cdot 048 \, \text{g}$

5.28   *(a)* $1 \cdot 20 \times 10^{24}$; *(b)* $2 \cdot 41 \times 10^{24}$

5.29 $0 \cdot 14 \, \text{g}$

5.30 $7 \cdot 31 \times 10^{-23} \, \text{g}$

5.31   *(a)* $3 \cdot 61 \times 10^{22}$; *(b)* $1 \cdot 08 \times 10^{23}$

5.32 $0 \cdot 0025 \, \text{g}$

5.33   *(a)* $9 \cdot 03 \times 10^{23}$; *(b)* $1 \cdot 20 \times 10^{24}$

5.34   *(a)* $3 \cdot 01 \times 10^{23}$; *(b)* $10 \, \text{g}$

5.35   *(a)* $9 \cdot 63 \times 10^{22}$; *(b)* $4 \cdot 82 \times 10^{22}$

5.36 $7 \cdot 97 \times 10^{-23} \, \text{g}$

5.37 $1 \cdot 63 \times 10^{-4} \, \text{g}$

5.38 $7 \cdot 22 \times 10^{21}$

5.39 $2 \cdot 17 \times 10^{23}$

5.40 $0 \cdot 068 \, \text{g}$

5.41 $2 \cdot 41 \times 10^{23}$

5.42 $1 \cdot 6 \, \text{mol} \, l^{-1}$

5.43 $50 \, \text{cm}^3$

5.44   *(a)* $6 \cdot 02 \times 10^{22}$; *(b)* $3 \cdot 01 \times 10^{22}$

5.45 $0 \cdot 05 \, \text{mol} \, l^{-1}$

5.46 $8 \, \text{cm}^3$

5.47   *(a)* $4 \cdot 33 \times 10^{23}$; *(b)* $1 \cdot 44 \times 10^{23}$

5.48 $0 \cdot 0625 \, \text{mol} \, l^{-1}$

5.49 $24 \, \text{cm}^3$

5.50 $0 \cdot 04 \, \text{mol} \, l^{-1}$

5.51 $0 \cdot 05 \, \text{mol} \, l^{-1}$

5.52 $2 \cdot 41 \times 10^{22}$

5.53 $25 \, \text{cm}^3$

5.54 $9 \cdot 63 \times 10^{21}$

5.55 $0 \cdot 02 \, \text{mol} \, l^{-1}$

5.56 $7 \cdot 22 \times 10^{21}$

5.57 $0 \cdot 015 \, \text{mol} \, l^{-1}$

5.58 $6 \cdot 25 \, \text{cm}^3$

5.59 $0 \cdot 1 \, \text{mol} \, l^{-1}$

5.60 NH_4^+: $2 \cdot 17 \times 10^{21}$; SO_4^{2-}: $1 \cdot 08 \times 10^{21}$

5.61 $5 \cdot 42 \times 10^{21}$

5.62 $0 \cdot 408 \, \text{g} \, l^{-1}$

5.63 $17 \cdot 9 \, \text{cm}^3$

5.64 34

5.65 $1 \cdot 05 \, \text{g} \, l^{-1}$

5.66 $2 \cdot 75 \times 10^{21}$

5·67 $1 \cdot 20 \times 10^{21}$

5.68 $93 \cdot 3 \, \text{cm}^3$

5·69 $1 \cdot 28 \, \text{g} \, l^{-1}$

5.70 $5 \cdot 45 \times 10^{22}$

5.71 $44 \cdot 1$

5.72 $1 \cdot 44 \times 10^{21}$

5.73 $9 \cdot 09 \, \text{cm}^3$

5.74 $1 \cdot 08 \times 10^{22}$

5.75 $31 \cdot 9$; O_2

5.76 $2 \cdot 8 \, l$

5.77 $1 \cdot 33 \, \text{g} \, l^{-1}$

5.78 $4 \cdot 40 \times 10^{21}$

5.79 $0 \cdot 638 \, \text{g} \, l^{-1}$ (rounded up from $0 \cdot 6375$)

5.80 $1 \cdot 56 \times 10^{22}$

CHAPTER 6 — Answers

Note that the answers are given to a maximum of 3 significant figures.

6. 1	0·119 g	**6. 2**	0·0555 g	**6. 3**	0·302 g
6. 4	0·00311 g	**6. 5**	(a) 3·09 g Pb; (b) 2·39 g Br_2	**6. 6**	(a) 0·00280 g H_2; (b) 0·0224 g O_2
6. 7	0·168 g	**6. 8**	(a) 0·00373 g H_2; (b) 0·0298 g O_2		
6. 9	597 g	**6.10**	806 kg	**6.11**	42·9 kg
6.12	13·2 kg	**6.13**	716 kg	**6.14**	1·29 kg
6.15	376 kg	**6.16**	643 minutes	**6.17**	0·402 A
6.18	0·268 A	**6.19**	483 minutes (482·5 rounded up)	**6.20**	32·2 minutes
6.21	3·22 A	**6.22**	1·61 A	**6.23**	172 minutes
6.24	0·483 A (0·4825 rounded up)	**6.25**	804 minutes	**6.26**	10 hours
6.27	$2·14 \times 10^3$ A (2140 A)	**6.28**	149 minutes	**6.29**	$1·79 \times 10^4$ A (17 900 A)
6.30	385 A	**6.31**	0·148 g (0·1475 rounded up)	**6.32**	0·32 g
6.33	10 g	**6.34**	0·2 g	**6.35**	2·36 g
6.36	4·16 g	**6.37**	1·97 g	**6.38**	0·768 g
6.39	0·06 g	**6.40**	0·54 g	**6.41**	2+
6.42	3+	**6.43**	3+	**6.44**	1+
6.45	2+				

CHAPTER 7 — Answers

7. 1	(a)	0·00108 g s^{-1} ($1·08 \times 10^{-3}$ g s^{-1})	(b)	0·0003 g s^{-1} (3×10^{-4} g s^{-1})
7. 2	(a)	0·00145 mol l^{-1} s^{-1} ($1·45 \times 10^{-3}$ mol l^{-1} s^{-1})	(b)	0·001 mol l^{-1} s^{-1} (1×10^{-3} mol l^{-1} s^{-1})
7. 3	(a)	0·8 cm^3 s^{-1}	(b)	0·2 cm^3 s^{-1}
7. 4	(a)	0·002 mol l^{-1} s^{-1} (2×10^{-3} mol l^{-1} s^{-1})	(b)	0·00068 mol l^{-1} s^{-1} ($6·8 \times 10^{-4}$ mol l^{-1} s^{-1})
7. 5	(a)	0·0125 g s^{-1} ($1·25 \times 10^{-2}$ g s^{-1})	(b)	0·0025 g s^{-1} ($2·5 \times 10^{-3}$ g s^{-1})
7. 6	(a)	0·5 cm^3 s^{-1}	(b)	0·12 cm^3 s^{-1}
7. 7	(a)	0·002 mol l^{-1} min^{-1} (2×10^{-3} mol l^{-1} min^{-1})	(b)	0·00064 mol l^{-1} min^{-1} ($6·4 \times 10^{-4}$ mol l^{-1} min^{-1})
7. 8	(a)	0·005 g s^{-1} (5×10^{-3} g s^{-1})	(b)	0·001875 g s^{-1} ($1·875 \times 10^{-3}$ g s^{-1})
7. 9	(a)	0·5 cm^3 s^{-1}	(b)	0·15 cm^3 s^{-1}
7.10	(a)	0·000096 mol l^{-1} s^{-1} ($9·6 \times 10^{-5}$ mol l^{-1} s^{-1})	(b)	0·00005 mol l^{-1} s^{-1} (5×10^{-5} mol l^{-1} s^{-1})
7.11	(a)	0·37 mol l^{-1}	(b)	50 s
7.12	(a)	25 s	(b)	33 °C
	(c)	0·004 s^{-1}, 0·008 s^{-1}, 0·016 s^{-1} and 0·032 s^{-1} respectively. The rate doubles with each 10 °C rise in temperature.		
7.13	(a)	0·32 mol l^{-1}	(b)	40 s
7.14	(a)	25 °C	(b)	25 s
7.15	(a)	62·5 s	(b)	0·0084 mol l^{-1}

CHAPTER 8 — Answers

NOTE: Where rounding has taken place, answers are given to a maximum of 3 significant figures.

8. 1	1	**8. 2**	1·30
8. 3	0·40	**8. 4**	7·21
8. 5	4·42	**8. 6**	1·70
8. 7	0·0969	**8. 8**	2
8. 9	1·40	**8.10**	−0·380
8.11	$3·16 \times 10^{-12}$ mol l^{-1}	**8.12**	$1·26 \times 10^{-13}$ mol l^{-1}
8.13	1·41 mol l^{-1}	**8.14**	$1·58 \times 10^{-5}$ mol l^{-1}
8.15	$3·16 \times 10^{-4}$ mol l^{-1}	**8.16**	(a) $1·58 \times 10^{-3}$ mol l^{-1} (b) $7·9 \times 10^{-4}$ mol l_{-1}
8.17	(a) 0·0316 mol l^{-1} (b) 0·0316 mol l^{-1}	**8.18**	(a) $6·31 \times 10^{-4}$ mol l^{-1} (b) $3·15 \times 10^{-4}$ mol l^{-1}
8.19	(a) 0·0158 mol l^{-1} (b) 0·0158 mol l^{-1}	**8.20**	(a) 1·58 mol l^{-1} (b) 0·79 mol l^{-1}
8.21	(a) 10^{-12} mol l^{-1} (b) 0·01 mol l^{-1}	**8.22**	(a) 4 (b) 10^{-10} mol l^{-1}
8.23	(a) 0·05 mol l^{-1} (b) 1·30	**8.24**	(a) $3·98 \times 10^{-9}$ mol l^{-1} (b) $2·51 \times 10^{-6}$ mol l^{-1}
8.25	(a) 2·47 (b) $2·94 \times 10^{-12}$ mol l^{-1}	**8.26**	(a) $1·59 \times 10^{-3}$ mol l^{-1} (b) 2·80
8.27	(a) 1·78 mol l^{-1} (b) $5·62 \times 10^{-15}$ mol l^{-1}	**8.28**	(a) 3·36 (b) $2·27 \times 10^{-11}$ mol l^{-1}
8.29	(a) 5×10^{-13} mol l^{-1} (b) 12·3	**8.30**	(a) $3·98 \times 10^{-4}$ mol l^{-1} (b) $2·51 \times 10^{-11}$ mol l^{-1}

CHAPTER 9 — Answers

Answers have been rounded to a **maximum** of 4 significant figures.

9. 1	3·344 kJ	**9. 2**	3·344 kJ	**9. 3**	3·135 kJ
9. 4	1·254 kJ	**9. 5**	39·71 kJ	**9. 6**	+167·2 kJ mol^{-1}
9. 7	−188·1 kJ mol^{-1}	**9. 8**	−334·4 kJ mol^{-1}	**9. 9**	−167·2 kJ mol^{-1}
9.10	+62·7 kJ mol^{-1}	**9.11**	−668·8 kJ mol^{-1}	**9.12**	−25·08 kJ mol^{-1}
9.13	−836 kJ mol^{-1}	**9.14**	+25·08 kJ mol^{-1}	**9.15**	−1338 kJ mol^{-1}
9.16	−41·8 kJ mol^{-1}	**9.17**	−2090 kJ mol^{-1}	**9.18**	+16·72 kJ mol^{-1}
9.19	−2665 kJ mol^{-1}	**9.20**	+33·44 kJ mol^{-1}	**9.21**	−58·52 kJ mol^{-1}
9.22	−57·68 kJ mol^{-1}	**9.23**	−56·85 kJ mol^{-1}	**9.24**	−56·85 kJ mol^{-1}
9.25	−57·06 kJ mol^{-1}	**9.26**	3·925 g	**9.27**	0·4207 g
9.28	0·2955 °C	**9.29**	0·337 g	**9.30**	6·603 °C rise
9.31	10·55 °C	**9.32**	5·963 g	**9.33**	33·41 g
9.34	11·04 g	**9.35**	13·48 g	**9.36**	3·427 °C
9.37	6·854 °C	**9.38**	3·427 °C	**9.39**	3·427 °C
9.40	9·139 °C				

CHAPTER 10 — Answers

10. 1 -891 kJ mol^{-1}	**10. 2** -1561 kJ mol^{-1}	**10. 3** -104 kJ mol^{-1}
10. 4 -2222 kJ mol^{-1}	**10. 5** -129 kJ mol^{-1}	**10. 6** -1368 kJ mol^{-1}
10. 7 -484 kJ mol^{-1}	**10. 8** -316 kJ mol^{-1}	**10. 9** -3271 kJ mol^{-1}
10.10 $+231$ kJ mol^{-1}	**10.11** -417 kJ mol^{-1}	**10.12** -495 kJ mol^{-1}
10.13 -131 kJ mol^{-1}	**10.14** -71 kJ mol^{-1}	**10.15** -335 kJ mol^{-1}
10.16 -412 kJ mol^{-1}	**10.17** $+399$ kJ mol^{-1}	**10.18** $+776$ kJ mol^{-1}
10.19 -409 kJ mol^{-1}	**10.20** -5120 kJ mol^{-1}	

CHAPTER 11 — Answers

11. 1 -631 kJ mol^{-1}	**11. 2** -630 kJ mol^{-1}	**11. 3** -122 kJ mol^{-1}
11. 4 -100 kJ mol^{-1}	**11. 5** -17 kJ mol^{-1}	**11. 6** -139 kJ mol^{-1}
11. 7 -69 kJ mol^{-1}	**11. 8** $+25$ kJ mol^{-1}	**11. 9** -919 kJ mol^{-1}
11.10 -547 kJ mol^{-1}	**11.11** $+11$ kJ mol^{-1}	**11.12** -307 kJ mol^{-1}
11.13 $+210$ kJ mol^{-1}	**11.14** -145 kJ mol^{-1}	**11.15** -746 kJ mol^{-1}
11.16 $-1083 \cdot 5$ kJ mol^{-1}	**11.17** $+9$ kJ mol^{-1}	**11.18** -78 kJ mol^{-1}
11.19 -20 kJ mol^{-1}	**11.20** -300 kJ mol^{-1}	

CHAPTER 12 — Answers

Answers are given to numerical parts of questions only.

12. 1 (b) $\Delta H1 = +121 \cdot 5$ kJ mol^{-1}; $\Delta H2 = +425$ kJ mol^{-1} (c) -708 kJ mol^{-1}

12. 2 (b) $\Delta H2 = +77 \cdot 5$ kJ mol^{-1}; $\Delta H3 = +409$ kJ mol^{-1} (c) $-534 \cdot 5$ kJ mol^{-1}

12. 3 (b) $\Delta H2 = +77 \cdot 5$ kJ mol^{-1}; $\Delta H3 = +526$ kJ mol^{-1} (c) $\Delta H5 = -1044$ kJ mol^{-1}

12. 4 (b) $\Delta H2 = +243$ kJ mol^{-1}; $\Delta H3 = +744$ kJ mol^{-1} $\Delta H4 = +1460$ kJ mol^{-1} (c) $+128$ kJ mol^{-1}

12. 5 (a) $\Delta H2 = +243$ kJ mol^{-1}; $\Delta H3 = +596$ kJ mol^{-1} $\Delta H4 = +1160$ kJ mol^{-1} (b) $\Delta H1 = -768$ kJ mol^{-1}

12. 6 (b) -37 kJ mol^{-1}

12. 7 (b) -344 kJ mol^{-1}

12. 8 (b) $+5$ kJ mol^{-1}

12. 9 -1586 kJ mol^{-1}

12.10 -84 kJ mol^{-1}

CHAPTER 13 — Answers

13. 1 4 days	**13. 2** 56 hours	**13. 3** 16 counts min^{-1}
13. 4 $2 \cdot 5$ years	**13. 5** $24 \cdot 9$ days	**13. 6** 1/32
13. 7 5 minutes	**13. 8** 21 s	**13. 9** $0 \cdot 0625$ g
13.10 $1 \cdot 2$ hours	**13.11** 24 s	**13.12** 25%
13.13 15 hours	**13.14** 840 days	**13.15** 1/16
13.16 $12 \cdot 3$ years	**13.17** $49 \cdot 8$ hours	**13.18** $3 \cdot 125$%
13.19 3×10^5 years	**13.20** $5 \cdot 2 \times 10^9$ years	**13.21** 11 140 years
13.22 4 counts min^{-1}	**13.23** 27 850 years	**13.24** 16 710 years
13.25 22 280 years		

CHAPTER 14 — Answers

14. 1	0·5 g	**14. 2**	12·8 g	**14. 3**	0·6 g
14. 4	3·5 g	**14. 5**	11·5 g	**14. 6**	0·4 g
14. 7	7·2 g	**14. 8**	2·2 g	**14. 9**	66 g
14.10	1·28 g	**14.11**	128 kg	**14.12**	37·5 kg
14.13	44·8 kg	**14.14**	960 kg	**14.15**	672 kg
14.16	$2·76 \times 10^3$ kg	**14.17**	$3·52 \times 10^4$ kg	**14.18**	$3·68 \times 10^3$ kg
14.19	$1·9 \times 10^5$ kg	**14.20**	$8·8 \times 10^3$ kg	**14.21**	840 kg ($8·4 \times 10^2$ kg)
14.22	1344 kg	**14.23**	$4·5 \times 10^3$ kg	**14.24**	28·99 kg
14.25	$1·728 \times 10^3$ kg	**14.26**	$7·14 \times 10^4$ kg	**14.27**	27·6 kg
14.28	$5·76 \times 10^4$ kg	**14.29**	$6·48 \times 10^3$ kg	**14.30**	6·66 g
14.31	(a) 256 kg; (b) 75%	**14.32**	40%	**14.33**	60%
14.34	75%	**14.35**	60%	**14.36**	65%
14.37	(a) 4·24 g; (b) 80%	**14.38**	86%	**14.39**	(a) 5·04 g; (b) 80%
14.40	64%				

CHAPTER 15 — Answers

15. 1	0·5 mol l^{-1}	**15. 2**	16 cm^3
15. 3	1·725 g	**15. 4**	300 cm^3
15. 5	0·8 mol l^{-1}	**15. 6**	4·15 g
15. 7	0·182 mol l^{-1}	**15. 8**	1·165 g
15. 9	0·094 mol l^{-1}	**15.10**	0·2 mol l^{-1}
15.11	0·0584 mol l^{-1}	**15.12**	0·2 mol l^{-1}
15.13	0·36 mol l^{-1}	**15.14**	0·12 mol l^{-1}
15.15	0·021 mol l^{-1}	**15.16**	(a) 0·2 mol l^{-1}; (b) 10 times; (c) 2 mol l^{-1}
15.17	(a) 2 mol l^{-1}; (b) 100 cm^3	**15.18**	(a) 0·125 mol l^{-1}; (b) 0·2 mol l^{-1}
15.19	(a) 100 times; (b) 0·025 mol l^{-1}; (c) 2·5 mol l^{-1}	**15.20**	(a) 0·02 mol; (b) 0·04 mol l^{-1}; (c) 0·04 mol l^{-1}
15.21	0·05 g	**15.22**	4·4 g
15.23	11·064 g	**15.24**	1·1 g
15.25	(a) 0·6 g; (b) 2 g	**15.26**	0·2583 g
15.27	0·932 g	**15.28**	0·85 g
15.29	1·36 g	**15.30**	1·56 g
15.31	50 cm^3	**15.32**	16 cm^3
15.33	0·0625 mol l^{-1}	**15.34**	40 cm^3
15.35	0·08 mol l^{-1}	**15.36**	0·05 mol l^{-1}
15.37	0·4 mol l^{-1}	**15.38**	18 cm^3
15.39	20 cm^3	**15.40**	38·4 cm^3

CHAPTER 16 — Answers

16. 1 (a) O_2; (b) 100 cm³ O_2 and 100 cm³ CO_2 **16. 2** (a) CO; (b) 40 cm³ CO_2 and 10 cm³ CO

16. 3 60 l CO_2 and 40 l O_2 **16. 4** 1200 l CO_2 and 3200 l O_2

16. 5 400 cm³ CO_2, 600 cm³ H_2O and 1300 cm³ O_2 **16. 6** 100 l N_2, 200 l H_2O and 300 l O_2

16. 7 600 l CO_2, 1025 l O_2 **16. 8** (a) $2 \cdot 4 \times 10^5$ l CO_2; (b) $5 \cdot 2 \times 10^5$ l H_2

16. 9 5×10^5 l CCl_4, 5×10^5 l S_2Cl_2, 10^6 l Cl_2 **16.10** $4 \cdot 5 \times 10^5$ l

CHAPTER 17 — Answers

17. 1 90 l **17. 2** $1 \cdot 1$ l **17. 3** 272 g

17. 4 320 l **17. 5** $2 \cdot 6$ g   **17. 6** $4 \cdot 4$ l

17. 7 40 000 l (4×10^4 l)   **17. 8** 80 kg   **17. 9** 3 l

17.10 234 kg

CHAPTER 18 — Answers

18. 1 (a) $6 \cdot 02 \times 10^{21}$; (b) $4 \cdot 515 \times 10^{21}$ **18. 2** $4 \cdot 816 \times 10^{22}$

18. 3 $9 \cdot 632 \times 10^{22}$ **18. 4** $0 \cdot 25$ g

18. 5 $4 \cdot 816 \times 10^{22}$ **18. 6** $3 \cdot 612 \times 10^{22}$

18. 7 $2 \cdot 408 \times 10^{22}$ **18. 8** $0 \cdot 0792$ g

18. 9 $0 \cdot 04$ mol l^{-1} **18.10** $442 \cdot 5$ g

18.11 $0 \cdot 006$ g   **18.12** $7 \cdot 224 \times 10^{22}$

18.13 $17 \cdot 25$ g   **18.14** (a) sodium carbonate in excess; (b) $4 \cdot 816 \times 10^{22}$

18.15 (a) ethanoic acid in excess; (b) $1 \cdot 204 \times 10^{22}$

NOTES

NOTES

NOTES

Printed by Bell & Bain Ltd., Glasgow.